Practical Faster Reading

Practical Faster Reading

A course in reading and vocabulary for
upper-intermediate and more advanced students

Gerald Mosback
Vivienne Mosback

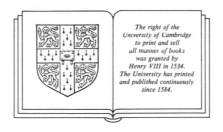

*The right of the
University of Cambridge
to print and sell
all manner of books
was granted by
Henry VIII in 1534.
The University has printed
and published continuously
since 1584.*

Cambridge University Press
Cambridge
London   New York   New Rochelle
Melbourne   Sydney

Published by the Press Syndicate of the University of Cambridge
The Pitt Building, Trumpington Street, Cambridge CB2 1RP
32 East 57th Street, New York, NY 10022, USA
10 Stamford Road, Oakleigh, Melbourne 3166, Australia

© Cambridge University Press 1976

First Published 1976
Ninth printing 1986

Printed in Great Britain at the
University Press, Cambridge

Library of Congress cataloguing in publication data
Mosback, Gerald Peter.
Practical reading: an intermediate/advanced course in reading and vocabulary.
(Cambridge English language learning)
1. English language–Text-books for foreigners.
I. Mosback, Vivienne, 1938- joint author. II. Title.
PE1128.M74   -428.2 4   76-12918
ISBN 0 521 21346 0

Contents

Preface

The reading practice offered by this course draws on a wide variety of general knowledge topics. The final selection is the result of several major revisions in the course of extensive use of the materials in a number of university, adult education and senior secondary school contexts, where English is the medium of instruction for non-native speakers. Experience suggests the course is best used as one element in a general scheme of work in English, and covered at a rate of one or two hours per week.

The passages are of approximately equal length (500 words) and the same level of difficulty throughout, to allow a really meaningful comparison of reading speeds and comprehension scores at the beginning and end of the course. In practice, reading speed improvement has been found to be in the region of 80–100% over 30–40 hours of instruction, but equally important has been the improvement in comprehension and extension of vocabulary resulting from other elements of the course.

The vocabulary level basically corresponds to level 5 of the *Cambridge English Lexicon,* and is entirely within the 5,000 words of the *Ladder* vocabulary, developed initially by the United States Information Service, both of which were closely consulted during preparation of the material. The Thorndike and Lorge *Teacher's Wordbook of 30,000 words* (Columbia University Press) was also consulted.

Words which fall outside the CEL level 5 are occasionally explained for the student, where such words are not semantically contextualized and the reader has no way of working out the meaning. Sometimes, however, such a word is the subject of a vocabulary question and is therefore not glossed.

We should like to thank the many teachers who used these materials in the experimental stage – particularly Janet James at the United Nations Economic Commission for Africa Headquarters, and John Murray-Robertson and Michael James, British Council instructors at the General Wingate School, Addis Ababa.

G. M.
V. M.

Acknowledgements

The author and publisher are grateful to the following for permission to reproduce quoted passages: Oxford University Press for passages 9, 10, 13, 15, 16, 17, 18, 19, 20, 27, 28 from the *Oxford Junior Encyclopedia*; William Collins & Son for passage 14 from Ann L. Stubbs, *Your Cat*; the American Medical Association for passages 21, 22 and 23 from *Today's Health Guide*.

How to use this book

Students should be aware at the outset that this is not exclusively a speed reading course. Reading practice courses to date have tended to fall into two sharply distinct categories – those which concentrate almost entirely on reading for speed, and those which seek to encourage comprehension at some leisure and in depth. This book is designed to improve the reading of expository English in two ways. It should certainly increase reading speed, through the first 'Ideas' exercises, but it should also improve comprehension in the areas of vocabulary, sentence patterns and paragraph structure through all the subsequent exercises.

Ideas

The reading *speed* element is covered by this section. The best method is to begin each reading practice session with the speed/ideas exercise. Since the passages are all approximately 500 words long, timing is simple. The teacher should make sure he has a watch with a seconds hand or a stop-watch. He marks up on the blackboard the passing of each ten seconds. As the student finishes reading and turns to the Ideas questions, he notes down the last time the teacher has written on the board. The values for a 500-word passage are roughly as follows:

Reading time (min/secs)	Speed (w.p.m.)	Reading time (min/secs)	Speed (w.p.m.)
1.00	500	3.10	158
1.10	427	3.20	150
1.20	375	3.30	143
1.30	334	3.40	137
1.40	300	3.50	131
1.50	273	4.00	125
2.00	250	4.10	120
2.10	231	4.20	116
2.20	215	4.30	111
2.30	200	4.40	107
2.40	188	4.50	104
2.50	174	5.00	100
3.00	167		

Students should answer the Ideas questions without looking back to the passage and in as short a time as possible. Five or six minutes should be enough to answer these questions so that the whole speed section, a reading of the passage and answering the Ideas questions should not take more than ten minutes altogether.

The students should keep a record in a convenient place of their reading time and Ideas score for each session. The Ideas score should not fall below 6 or 7 out of 10, while a steady and encouraging improvement should be noted in the speed. The passages are definitely not designed for lecture/ explanation presentation in the first instance, and bearing in mind that a reading speed of 250 w.p.m. is at the low end of the scale for an educated native speaker dealing with this kind of material at upper high school and college level, ESL students should certainly not take more than three to four minutes for a passage, with comprehension at around 70%. Initially, students will probably underestimate the time they need to read a passage under the mistaken impression that *speed* is the only important object of the exercise. It must be remembered that mere speed without retention is valueless.

Note that although units 1–4 are the same in length and format as all other units in the book, the passage content forms a revision of points relating to the process of reading speed improvement and should be re-read and explained with care by the teacher. If he wishes to time one or more of them for familiarization and as a check on students' reading speeds at the beginning of the course, care should be taken to go over the passage again in detail on completion of the exercise. Since this is an upper-intermediate to advanced course, however, it is expected that most students will already be familiar with many of the points covered in units 1–4.

Vocabulary

As far as possible, the vocabulary questions are designed to provide not only a contextually identifiable *correct* answer, but, in addition, to expand the student's vocabulary by including secondary and related meanings among the distractors. The student *must* look back to the passage for this exercise, as only the context will tell him which of the possible meanings of a word is the correct one for the passage. In many instances the student may be definitely misled if he does not look back. In passage 22, Vocabulary, for example:

roughly (line 2)
a) approximately
b) crudely
c) impolitely
d) exactly

the correct answer for this context, a), is probably no more common a meaning for 'roughly' in general English than either b) or c). This is an area where the teacher can considerably expand the students' recognition vocabulary when he discusses the answers with the class. Shades of meaning between apparent synonyms, prefix, suffix and root meanings can be explored. Of course it is not possible for all the distractors to be relevant in this way since the number of words with four or more meanings is limited, but the opportunity has been taken wherever possible, and it is just as important to explain why the wrong answers are wrong as why the right answers are correct. Certainly the teacher should not be content merely to read off, or have the students read off, the list of correct answers.

Similar or different?

This exercise brings the student from word level to phrase and sentence level in close reading practice. Under the teacher's guidance, and with reference to the passage, he will consolidate his understanding of relationships between the more common sentence patterns in English.

Missing word summary

With this exercise, the focus widens still further to the relationship between sentences within the paragraph. In each exercise, five of the missing words are structural and five contextualized vocabulary.

Spot the topic

Here the student's attention is drawn to the thematic nature of the English paragraph, and the total effect in combination of its component sentences.

Discussion and writing topics

Towards the end of the course (passages 26–30) discussion and writing topics are introduced. These are designed for the most general use possible, either for oral work with smaller groups, or writing practice after class preparation by the teacher. They broaden the scope of the course towards the end to lead on to more general work when sound reading habits have been firmly established.

All the later exercises should be worked through with as much guidance from the teacher as necessary. We should like to emphasize that only the Ideas questions are concerned with checking the reading *speed* practice. The remaining exercises should be covered in detail and with care.

Introductory passages 1–4

Note to students

Passages 1–4 revise points you may have covered in preliminary reading courses, but they may include some new hints. Read these passages carefully. They will also serve to familiarize you with the layout of the passages and questions for the speed reading practice in passages 5–30.

Introductory passage 1

Faster effective reading

The comprehension passages on this course are designed to help you
increase your reading speed. A higher reading rate, with no loss of
comprehension, will help you in other subjects as well as English, and
the general principles apply to any language. Naturally, you will not read
every book at the same speed. You would expect to read a newspaper,   5
for example, much more rapidly than a physics or economics textbook –
but you can raise your *average* reading speed over the whole range of
materials you wish to cover so that the percentage gain will be the same
whatever kind of reading you are concerned with.

The reading passages which follow are all of an average level of diffi-   10
culty for your stage of instruction. They are all approximately 500 words
long. They are about topics of general interest which do not require a
great deal of specialized knowledge. Thus they fall between the kind of
reading you might find in your textbooks and the much less demanding
kind you will find in a newspaper or light novel. If you read *this* kind   15
of English, with understanding, at, say, 400 words per minute, you might
skim through a newspaper at perhaps 650–700, while with a difficult
textbook you might drop to 200 or 250.

Perhaps you would like to know what reading speeds are common
among native English-speaking university students and how those speeds   20
can be improved. Tests in Minnesota, U.S.A., for example, have shown
that students without special training can read English of average difficulty,
for example Tolstoy's *War and Peace* in translation, at speeds of between
240 and 250 w.p.m. with about 70% comprehension. Minnesota claims
that after 12 half-hour lessons, one a week, the reading speed can be   25
increased, with no loss of comprehension, to around 500 w.p.m. It is
further claimed that with intensive training over seventeen weeks, speeds of
over 1000 w.p.m. can be reached, but this would be quite exceptional.

If you get to the point where you can read books of average difficulty
at between 400 and 500 w.p.m. with 70% or more comprehension, you   30
will be doing quite well, though of course any further improvement of
speed-with-comprehension will be a good thing.

In this and the following three passages we shall be looking at some
of the obstacles to faster reading and what we can do to overcome them.

Think of the passage as a whole

When you practise reading with passages shorter than book length, like   35
the passages in this course, do not try to take in each word separately,
one after the other. It is much more difficult to grasp the broad theme
of the passage this way, and you will also get stuck on individual words
which may not be absolutely essential to a general understanding of the
passage. It is a good idea to skim through the passage very quickly first   40
(say 500 words in a minute or so) to get the general idea of each paragraph.
Titles, paragraph headings and emphasized words (underlined or in italics)
can be a great help in getting this skeleton outline of the passage. It is
surprising how many people do not read titles, introductions or paragraph
headings. Can you, *without* looking back, remember the title of this   45
passage and the heading of this paragraph?

Ideas

Select the answer which is most accurate according to the information
given in the passage.

1   A higher reading rate will help in other subjects as well as English
a) provided there is no loss of understanding.
b) only if we memorize well.
c) but not in any other language.
d) though not as a general principle.

2   You would expect to read a difficult economics textbook
a) as fast as you read a newspaper.
b) more slowly than you read a newspaper.
c) more quickly than you read these passages.
d) only very rarely.

3   You can expect to read the passages on this course
a) more **quickly** than you read your textbooks.
b) more quickly than you read a newspaper.
c) more slowly than you read your textbooks.
d) faster than any other kind of material.

4   The average untrained native speaker at the University of Minnesota
a) reads at 600 w.p.m.
b) reads at about 300 w.p.m.
c) cannot read difficult works in translation.
d) reads at about 245 w.p.m.

5   The University of Minnesota claims that in 12 half-hour lessons
a) it can triple a student's reading speed.
b) it can double a student's reading speed.
c) it can increase a student's reading speed four times.
d) no real increase in reading speed can be achieved.

6 Intensive training over seventeen weeks can
a) triple an untrained student's reading speed.
b) increase an untrained student's reading speed four times.
c) double an untrained student's reading speed.
d) triple the students' comprehension scores.

7 You will be doing quite well if you can read books of average difficulty
a) at about 450 w.p.m. with 70% comprehension.
b) at about 600 w.p.m. with 60% comprehension.
c) at about 300 w.p.m. with 70% comprehension.
d) at about 250 w.p.m. with 50% comprehension.

8 Reading words one at a time is bad because
a) it hurts your eyes.
b) all words are equally important.
c) it is more difficult to get the general idea of a passage.
d) some words are longer than others.

9 It is a good idea to skim through a passage quickly first
a) at about 350 w.p.m.
b) to get the general idea of each paragraph.
c) so that you can take in each word separately.
d) to make sure you get to the end at least once.

10 Titles and paragraph headings
a) are more important than anything else.
b) are surprising to many people.
c) can easily be remembered without looking back.
d) can help us get the outline of a passage.

Vocabulary

Find the following words in the passage and select the meaning you think
is *most likely* to correspond among the choices given.

1 *rate* (line 2)
a) speed
b) tax
c) score
d) awareness

2 *naturally* (line 4)
a) easily
b) unfortunately
c) without training
d) of course

3 *range* (line 7)
a) distance
b) variety
c) territory
d) farm

4 *demanding* (line 14)
a) difficult
b) questioning
c) insisting
d) asking

5 *skim through* (line 17)
a) read quickly through
b) make smooth with
c) concentrate on
d) strain through

8) *take in* (line 36)
a) understand
b) adjust
c) memorize
d) say

6 *native* (line 20)
a) unsophisticated
b) primitive
c) taught from childhood
d) uneducated

9 *grasp* (line 37)
a) grip tightly
b) understand
c) hold loosely
d) avoid

7 *obstacles* (line 34)
a) prohibitions
b) hindrances
c) objections
d) disadvantages

10 *italics* (line 42)
a) brackets
b) margins
c) sloping letters
d) smaller print

Spot the topic

Which of the following choices a), b) or c), most adequately sums up the ideas of the *whole* paragraph?

1 *Para. 1* (lines 1–9)
a) How to increase your reading speed.
b) The advantages of a generally higher reading speed.
c) The advantages to your English of a higher reading speed.

2 *Para. 2* (lines 10–18)
a) The interest of the reading passages in this course.
b) Newspapers can be read more quickly than textbooks.
c) The speed at which you might expect to read different types of English.

3 *Para. 3* (lines 19–28)
a) How native English speakers read faster than others.
b) How speed reading courses affected students' reading speeds.
c) How native English university students increased their reading speed to 1000 w.p.m. on average.

4 *Para. 4* (lines 29–32)
a) A guide to the reading speed you could aim for.
b) The point of reading books of average difficulty.
c) Why further improvement is a good thing.

5 *Para. 6* (lines 35–end)
a) Advice on how to get the general idea of a piece of reading quickly.
b) The use of the title.
c) The disadvantage of too careful initial reading.

Obstacles to faster effective reading

Perhaps you have seen very young children – or very old people – learning
to read. They move the index finger along the line of print, pointing to
each word, sometimes even to individual letters, saying the word or letters
to themselves in a low voice. This is called 'vocalizing'. Sometimes the
learner makes no sound though his lips may move to form the words, some-   5
times there is not even any perceptible movement of the mouth at all, but
the learner is still activating his throat muscles slightly to 'say' the words
to himself. He is still vocalizing.

However slight the extent of vocalizing may be it will still be impossible
for such a reader to reach a speed of more than about 280 w.p.m. The   10
appreciation of written words must be entirely visual and we must read
more than one word at a time.

Look at 'you', the second word of this passage. Even if you look
straight at the 'o' of that word, without moving your eyes at all you can
clearly see 'perhaps' and 'have' on either side. So you can read three   15
words at once. Now look at the word 'word' on line 3. With a very slight
movement of the eyes, you can take in the whole phrase '...saying the
word or letters...' in the same glance. In the same way, you can probably
take in a complete short sentence on one line, like the one on line 8, at
one glance. None of the lines of print on a page this size should need more   20
than three eye movements. Take line 6. This would perhaps break up into
three word groups: (1)...times there is not even ....(2)...any perceptible
movement...(3)...of the mouth at all, but...When you are reading well,
your eyes will be one or two word groups ahead of the one your mind is
taking in.   25

Practise on something easy and interesting

Many students trying to increase their effective reading speed become
discouraged when they find that if they try to race through a passage
faster, they fail to take in what they have read. At the end, they have
been so busy 'reading faster' that they cannot remember what the passage
was about. The problem here is that the material they are practising on   30
is either too difficult for them in vocabulary or content, or not sufficiently
interesting. We hope that the passages in this course material will be both
interesting and fairly easy, but you should also practise as much as you
can in your own time. Read things you like reading. Go to the subject
catalogue in the library. Biography, sport, domestic science, the cinema...   35

there is bound to be some area that interests you and in which you can find books of about your level of ability or just below.

If you want a quick check on how easy a book is, read through three or four pages at random. If there are, on average, more than five or six words on each page that are completely new to you, then the book (though you may persevere with it for interest's sake) is not suitable for reading-speed improvement. Incidentally, you should try to read three or four times as much 'light' speed reading material (whether it is *Newsweek, The Saint* or *A Tale of Two Cities*) as you do close, slow textbook work. You cannot achieve a permanent improvement in your reading speed if most of the time you are practising reading slowly.

40

45

Ideas

Say whether the following statements are true or false according to the information given in the passage.

1 Very old people and very young children learn to read in much the same way.
2 Vocalizing will prevent readers from reading at speeds of over 100 w.p.m.
3 It is sometimes possible to see three words at once without moving the eyes.
4 To read well your eyes should be one or two word groups ahead of mind.
5 Some students get discouraged when they first start reading faster.
6 It is more important to read fast than to understand what is read.
7 Reading practice material should be interesting and not too hard.
8 It is impossible to check quickly how difficult a book is.
9 You should never read a book that has five or six new words per page.
10 *Newsweek, The Saint* and *A Tale of Two Cities* are unsuitable for students.

Vocabulary

Find the following words in the passage and select the meaning you think is *most likely* to correspond among the choices given.

1 *index finger* (line 2)
a) little finger
b) thumb
c) ring finger
d) first finger

2 *perceptible* (line 6)
a) observable
b) loud
c) excessive
d) piercing

3 *activating* (line 7)
a) restraining
b) feeling
c) operating
d) acting

4 *appreciation* (line 11)
a) approval
b) satisfaction
c) perception
d) increase

5 *glance* (line 18)
a) look
b) line
c) breath
d) stance

6 *discouraged* (line 27)
a) interested
b) disabled
c) dissatisfied
d) courageous

7 *race* (line 27)
a) hurry
b) compete
c) concentrate
d) read carefully

8 *content* (line 31)
a) satisfaction
b) ideas
c) amount
d) pleasure

9 *area* (line 36)
a) space
b) extent
c) subject
d) width

10 *persevere with* (line 41)
a) try hard with
b) dispense with
c) dispose of
d) despair of

Missing word summary

Fill in the numbered blanks from the selection of words given below. The correct choices will complete the sense of this summary of the reading passage.

You only read slowly if you [1] or look at individual words or letters. To improve reading speeds, your eye must [2] groups of words swiftly [3] your mind is absorbing the ideas. One [4] of practising faster reading is that you may not remember the ideas. This [5] be because the English is too [6] for this type of practice. Choose a book with, on average [7] than six new words per page.

1 a) glance
   b) vocalize
   c) pronunciation

2 a) take in
   b) take over
   c) take on

3 a) unless
   b) while
   c) after

4 a) advantage
   b) method
   c) danger

5 a) is
   b) has
   c) may

6 a) easy
   b) difficult
   c) unlikely

7 a) fewer
   b) more
   c) at least

Hints for reading practice (part 1)

Set aside time each day

Most of us can find 15 minutes or half an hour each day for some specific
regular activity. It may be a free period or a regular wait, say in the queue
for a bus or meal – even while eating breakfast. One famous surgeon always
made it a rule to spend at least 15 minutes on general reading before he
went to sleep each night. Whether he went to bed at 10 p.m. or 2.30 a.m.   5
made no difference. Even if you cannot keep to this kind of discipline, it
is a good idea to make sure you always have a general interest book in
your pocket. Don't forget it should be a book which entertains you and
the English must not be too difficult for you.

Check your progress through pacing

Nearly all 'speed reading' courses have a 'pacing' element – some timing   10
device which lets the student know how many words a minute he is
reading. You can do this simply by looking at your watch every 5 or 10
minutes and noting down the page number you have reached. Check the
average number of words per page for the particular book you are reading.
How do you know when 5 minutes have passed on your watch if you are   15
busy reading the book? Well, this is difficult at first. A friend can help by
timing you over a set period, or you can read within hearing distance of a
public clock which strikes the quarter hours. Pace yourself every three or
four days, always with the same kind of easy, general interest book. You
should soon notice your habitual w.p.m. rate creeping up.   20

Check comprehension

Obviously there is little point in increasing your w.p.m. rate if you do
not understand what you are reading. When you are consciously trying to
increase your reading speed, stop after every chapter (if you are reading a
novel) or every section or group of ten or twelve pages (if it is a textbook)
and ask yourself a few questions about what you have been reading. If   25
you find you have lost the thread of the story, or you cannot remember
clearly the details of what was said, re-read the section or chapter.

'Lightning speed' exercise

Try this from time to time. Take four or five pages of the general interest
book you happen to be reading at the time. *Read them as fast as you
possibly can.* Do not bother about whether you understand or not. Now   30
go back and read them at what you feel to be your 'normal' w.p.m. rate,
the rate at which you can comfortably understand. After a 'lightning speed'
read through (probably around 600 w.p.m.) you will usually find that
your 'normal' speed has increased – perhaps by as much as 50–100 w.p.m.
This is the technique athletes use when they habitually run further in   35
training than they will have to on the day of the big race.

Ideas

Select the answer which is most accurate according to the information
given in the passage.

1   The passage recommends setting aside for reading practice
a)   two hours a day.
b)   one hour a day.
c)   15 minutes or half an hour a day.
d)   three times a day before meals.

2   One famous surgeon always made it a rule to read
a)   for 15 minutes at 10 p.m. each night.
b)   at least 15 minutes at bedtime.
c)   at least 15 minutes at either 10 p.m. or 2.30 a.m.
d)   whenever he had a spare moment.

3   It is a good idea always to carry in your pocket
a)   a book you will never forget.
b)   a serious book.
c)   several books of various kinds.
d)   an easy and entertaining English book.

4   A 'pacing' device
a)   times a student's reading speed.
b)   is not included in most speed reading courses.
c)   is an aid to vocabulary learning.
d)   should be used whenever we read alone.

5   Looking at your watch every 5 or 10 minutes
a)   avoids the need for reading faster.
b)   is not the same as pacing.
c)   is not easy at first.
d)   helps you to remember the page number you were at last time.

6   The passage recommends pacing yourself
a)   every two days with different kinds of book.

b) every three or four days with the same kind of book.
c) every week with the same kind of book.
d) as often as you read a book.

7   When you are reading a novel the passage advises you to pause to check the content
a) every chapter.
b) every hour.
c) every three or four pages.
d) after every page.

8   The purpose of pausing for thought every so often is to
a) rest the eyes.
b) make sure you have not missed any pages.
c) make sure you really understand what you have read.
d) prevent brain fatigue.

9   If you have lost the thread of a story you are reading, the passage recommends
a) choosing an easier book.
b) glancing back over the chapter you have just read.
c) asking a friend to help you with the difficult words.
d) learning the previous chapter by heart.

10 The purpose of the lightning speed exercise is to
a) increase your normal speed by practising at a very high rate.
b) get through the book in half the time so that you can go on to the next.
c) help you understand more of the content of the book.
d) enable you to win reading races against your friends.

Vocabulary

Find the following words in the passage and select the meaning you think is *most likely* to correspond among the choices given.

1   *hints* (title)
a) tests
b) suggestions
c) obstacles
d) rewards

3   *specific* (line 1)
a) particular
b) uninteresting
c) specimen
d) intellectual

2   *set aside* (sub-title)
a) reject
b) put beside
c) push out of the way
d) allocate

4   *keep to* (line 6)
a) save
b) obey
c) protect
d) pay for

5 *pacing* (sub-title)	8 *set* (line 17)
a) hurrying	a) definite
b) reading faster	b) collection
c) checking w.p.m.	c) series
d) stepping carefully	d) hardened

6 *device* (line 11)	9 *consciously* (line 22)
a) means	a) awake
b) clamp	b) aware
c) symbol	c) purposefully
d) machine	d) regularly

7 *timing* (line 17)	10 *thread* (line 26)
a) co-ordinating	a) cotton
b) taking time with	b) step
c) checking the time taken by	c) sequence
d) estimating	d) beginning

Similar or different?

Say whether or not the statement is similar in meaning to the sentence from the passage indicated by the line number in brackets.

1 It is good to keep a general interest book in your pocket rather than reading at night. (lines 3–6)
2 Most reading courses incorporate a pacing device which permits the student to assess his reading speed. (lines 10–11)
3 Someone can tell you when so many minutes have passed, or you can hear a clock which strikes every 15 minutes. (lines 16–18)
4 There is hardly any point in increasing your reading speed provided that you understand what you are reading. (lines 21–22)
5 Read them with all speed, irrespective of understanding. (Two sentences, lines 29–30)
6 Athletes use 'lightning speed' reading exercises when they are in training for a big race. (lines 35–36)

Introductory passage 4

Hints for reading practice (part 2)

Dictionaries slow you down!

If you have chosen the right, fairly easy, sort of book for your general
reading practice, you will not need to use a dictionary for such an exercise.
If you really must know the dictionary meaning of all the words you meet
(a doubtful neccessity) jot them down on a piece of paper to look up later.
Actually, the meanings of many words will be clear from the sentences   5
around them – what we call the 'context'. Here is an example. Do you know
the word 'sou'wester'? It has two meanings in English as the following
sentences indicate:
a) In spite of the fact that the fishermen were wearing sou'westers, the
    storm was so heavy they were wet through.   10
b) An east or north-east wind brings cold, dry weather to England, but a
    sou'wester usually brings rain.
    You should have guessed very easily that in sentence a) the word
sou'wester refers to some kind of waterproof clothing, presumably quite
thick and heavy since it is worn by fishermen in storms. In sentence b)   15
it is clearly a kind of wind, coming from a *south*-westerly direction.
Incidentally, you would have had the greatest difficulty in *finding* this
word in most dictionaries since it often appears a long way down among
the secondary meanings of *south*. If you did not know that sou' meant
'south' in the first place you could only have found the word by the   20
merest chance.

Pay attention to paragraph structure

Most paragraphs have a 'topic sentence' which expresses the central idea.
The remaining sentences expand or support that idea. It has been estimated
that between 60 and 90% of all expository* paragraphs in English have the
topic sentence first. Always pay special attention to the first sentence of a   25
paragraph; it is most likely to give you the main idea.
    Sometimes, though, the first sentence in the paragraph does not have
the *feel* of a 'main idea' sentence. It does not seem to give us enough new
information to justify a paragraph. The next most likely place to look for
the topic sentence is the last sentence of the paragraph.   30
Take this paragraph for example:

* *expository*: giving information.

'Some students prefer a strict teacher who tells them exactly what to
do. Others prefer to be left to work on their own. Still others like a
democratic discussion type of class. No one teaching method can be
devised to satisfy all students at the same time.'   35

Remember that the opening and closing paragraphs of a passage or
chapter are particularly important. The opening paragraph suggests the
general direction and content of the piece, while the closing paragraph often
summarizes the very essence of what has been said.

Ideas

Select the answer which is most accurate according to the information given
in the passage.

1   The use of a dictionary is
a)   advisable for speed reading practice.
b)   unnecessary for speed reading practice.
c)   essential for speed reading practice.
d)   of no help in improving general reading ability.

2   You can avoid the need for reference books by
a)   learning many vocabulary items in advance.
b)   choosing a fairly easy book.
c)   asking a friend.
d)   simply ignoring unknown words.

3   If you really want to know what all the words mean
a)   make a note and check later.
b)   use a bigger dictionary.
c)   ask your instructor.
d)   read more slowly.

4   To understand a general reading book, a knowledge of the meaning of
every single word in that book is
a)   doubtfully necessary.
b)   absolutely unnecessary.
c)   absolutely necessary.
d)   most advisable.

5   Even if you don't know a word you can often get the meaning by
a)   wild guessing.
b)   working it out mathematically.
c)   working it out from the context.
d)   comparing it with similar words.

6   Words like *sou'wester* are often difficult even to *find* in a dictionary.
They may be
a)   spelled wrongly.
b)   listed under another word.

c) only put in by chance.
d) taken from another language.

7   The topic sentence of an expository paragraph in English
a) usually comes in the middle.
b) is most likely to be found at the end.
c) is most often at the beginning.
d) is usually omitted in expository writing.

8   Most expository paragraphs in English have a clearly defined topic
    sentence. In such paragraphs the topic sentence comes first
a) in about 40% of cases.
b) in about 80% of cases.
c) in about 20% of cases.
d) very rarely.

9   Sometimes we know the first sentence is not the topic sentence
    because
a) it does not seem to give us enough new information.
b) it is not long enough.
c) it does not come at the beginning.
d) it does not make complete sense.

10 The closing paragraph of a piece of writing
a) is not really very important.
b) is often unnecessary repetition.
c) often comes at the end.
d) often summarizes the essence of the passage.

Vocabulary

In the passage, you saw how it was possible to arrive at the two different
meanings of 'sou'wester' without having recourse to a dictionary. Each of
the words italicized in the following sentences is a word you will probably
not know. Simple equivalents for these words will be found among the
twelve words at the end of the exercise (you will not need two of them).
Try to work out from the context which words in the list replace the
italicized words in the sentences.

1   Many early types of human being were *troglodytes* before they learned
    to build houses.
2   Mohammed Ali was not fighting seriously in the gymnasium – he was
    only *sparring* with a friend.
3   The Prince left most of the ordinary everyday decisions to his *satraps*.
4   The crowd obviously enjoyed the fat man's *risible* efforts to compete
    in the 100 metres dash.
5   Italian artists were more active in the *quattrocento* than in the six-
    teenth century which followed.

6   General de Gaulle always wore a *képi* with his uniform instead of a
    steel helmet.
7   The Japanese are investigating the possibility of using marine resources
    such as plankton and *kelp* for human food.
8   The soldiers did not have plates so they ate straight from the *dixie*.
9   The politician was embarrassed when his argument was proved to be
    specious.
10 The fortune-teller was unable to *prognosticate* the events of the
    following week.

a) produce   e) stewpot   i) cave-dwellers
b) foretell   f) practising   j) amusing
c) illogical   g) deputies   k) fifteenth century
d) seaweed   h) hunters   l) peaked cap

Spot the topic

Which of the following choices a), b) or c) most adequately sums up the
ideas of the *whole* paragraph?

1   *Para. 1* (lines 1–8)
a) A dictionary is always a useful book to have at hand.
b) Context is a more useful indicator of meaning than a dictionary when
    you are speed reading.
c) If you jot down words on a slip of paper, you can look them up in a
    dictionary afterwards.

2   *Para. 2* (lines 9–21)
a) Sou'wester has *two* meanings.
b) Sou'wester is not easy to find in the dictionary.
c) An example of how contexts give meaning without recourse to the
    dictionary.

3   *Para. 3* (lines 22–6)
a) The function and usual place of the paragraph structure.
b) The function and usual place of the topic sentence.
c) What the topic sentence does.

4   *Para. 4* (lines 31–35)
a) The topic sentence is not always at the beginning of the paragraph.
b) An example of a non-final topic sentence in a paragraph.
c) An example of how a topic sentence can come at the end of a
    paragraph.

5   *Para. 5* (lines 36–39)
a) The importance of opening and closing sentences in a paragraph.
b) The importance of first and final paragraphs in a passage.
c) The importance of the general direction and content of a piece of
    writing.

Money

Aristotle, the Greek philosopher, summed up the four chief qualities of
money some 2,000 years ago. It must be lasting and easy to recognize, to
divide, and to carry about. In other words it must be, 'durable, distinct,
divisible and portable'. When we think of money today, we picture it
either as round, flat pieces of metal which we call coins, or as printed   5
paper notes. But there are still parts of the world today where coins and
notes are of no use. They will buy nothing, and a traveller might starve if
he had none of the particular local 'money' to exchange for food.

Among isolated peoples, who are not often reached by traders from
outside, commerce usually means barter. There is a direct exchange of   10
goods. Perhaps it is fish for vegetables, meat for grain, or various kinds of
food in exchange for pots, baskets, or other manufactured goods. For
this kind of simple trading, money is not needed, but there is often something that everyone wants and everybody can use, such as salt to flavour
food, shells for ornaments, or iron and copper to make into tools and   15
vessels. These things – salt, shells or metals – are still used as money in
out-of-the-way parts of the world today.

Salt may seem rather a strange substance to use as money, but in
countries where the food of the people is mainly vegetable, it is often
an absolute necessity. Cakes of salt, stamped to show their value, were   20
used as money in Tibet until recent times, and cakes of salt will still buy
goods in Borneo and parts of Africa.

Cowrie sea shells have been used as money at some time or another
over the greater part of the Old World. These were collected mainly from
the beaches of the Maldive Islands in the Indian Ocean, and were traded   25
to India and China. In Africa, cowries were traded right across the
continent from East to West. Four or five thousand went for one Maria
Theresa dollar, an Austrian silver coin which was once accepted as currency
in many parts of Africa.

Metal, valued by weight, preceded coins in many parts of the world.   30
Iron, in lumps, bars or rings is still used in many countries instead of
money. It can either be exchanged for goods, or made into tools, weapons
or ornaments. The early money of China, apart from shells, was of bronze,
often in flat, round pieces with a hole in the middle, called 'cash'. The
earliest of these are between three thousand and four thousand years old   35
– older than the earliest coins of the eastern Mediterranean.

Nowadays, coins and notes have supplanted nearly all the more
picturesque forms of money, and although in one or two of the more

remote countries people still hoard it for future use on ceremonial
occasions such as weddings and funerals, examples of primitive money 40
will soon be found only in museums.

Ideas

Select the answer which is most accurate according to the information given in
the passage.

1 Aristotle said money should be
a) made of metal.
b) durable, distinct, divisible and portable.
c) 2,000 years old.
d) made of high-quality materials.

2 Nowadays we think of money as
a) made of either metal or paper.
b) pieces of metal.
c) printed notepaper.
d) useful for starving travellers.

3 In some parts of the world a traveller might starve
a) even if his money was of the local kind.
b) even if he had no coins or notes.
c) if he did not know the local rate of exchange.
d) even if he had plenty of coins and notes.

4 Barter usually takes the place of money transactions where
a) there is only salt.
b) the people's trading needs are fairly simple.
c) metal tools are used.
d) money is unknown.

5 Salt is still used as money
a) in Tibet.
b) in the Maldive Islands.
c) in several countries.
d) only for ceremonial purposes.

6 Four or five thousand cowrie shells used to be
a) as valuable as a Maria Theresa dollar.
b) valued because they were easy to carry.
c) useful currency in South America.
d) the maximum one man could carry.

7 Lumps of iron or iron bars are
a) a substitute for money in some places.
b) never exchanged for goods nowadays.
c) exchanged for tools, weapons or ornaments.
d) called 'cash' in China.

8   One type of early Chinese money was
a)   made from bones.
b)   called 'cash'.
c)   better than eastern Mediterranean coins.
d)   in the form of bronze bars.

9   The earliest known coins from the eastern Mediterranean
a)   are as old as the earliest known Chinese coins.
b)   are older than the earliest known Chinese coins.
c)   are not as old as the earliest known Chinese coins.
d)   were much larger than their Chinese equivalents.

10   Primitive types of money are sometimes used
a)   to replace more picturesque forms.
b)   in museums, as entrance fees.
c)   at country markets.
d)   at weddings and funerals.

Vocabulary

Find the following words in the passage and select the meaning you think
is *most likely* to correspond among the choices given.

1   *some* (line 2)
a)   approximately
b)   not as many as
c)   a few more than
d)   a little

2   *distinct* (line 3)
a)   recognizable
b)   separate
c)   portable
d)   long-lasting

3   *particular* (line 8)
a)   exact
b)   careful
c)   special
d)   fussy

4   *outside* (line 10)
a)   other countries
b)   nearby villages
c)   the interior
d)   the open air

5   *direct* (line 10)
a)   honest
b)   simple
c)   ordered
d)   hurried

6   *substance* (line 18)
a)   material
b)   weightiness
c)   body
d)   content

7   *stamped* (line 20)
a)   pressed down
b)   trodden upon
c)   cut
d)   imprinted

8   *supplanted* (line 37)
a)   given way to
b)   replaced
c)   been superseded by
d)   been buried in the ground

9 *picturesque* (line 38)
a) bearing a picture
b) painted by artists
c) unusually attractive
d) mountainous

10 *hoard* (line 39)
a) store
b) display
c) spend
d) waste

Missing word summary

Fill in the numbered blanks from the selection of words given below. The correct choices will complete the sense of this summary of the reading passage.

[1] the important qualities for money were defined 2,000 years [2], there are still places in the world where practical coins and notes have not been adopted. Where trading needs are simple, [3] is sometimes used. Cakes of salt, imprinted with their value, [4] still another [5] form of money in some places. Four or five thousand cowrie shells [6] worth one silver dollar. These strange examples of money, [7], are found [8] in the modern world.

1 a) If
   b) When
   c) Although

2 a) before
   b) before Christ
   c) ago

3 a) the exchange rate
   b) barter
   c) a cheque

4 a) is
   b) are
   c) have been

5 a) currently
   b) currency
   c) current

6 a) used to be
   b) were used
   c) used to

7 a) although
   b) moreover
   c) however

8 a) less and less
   b) frequently
   c) less rarely

Passage 6

Diamonds

Some of the earliest diamonds known came from India. In the eighteenth century they were found in Brazil, and in 1866, huge deposits were found near Kimberley in South Africa. Though evidence of extensive diamond deposits has recently been found in Siberia, the continent of Africa still produces nearly all the world's supply of these stones.   5

The most valuable diamonds are large, individual crystals of pure crystalline carbon. Less perfect forms, known as 'boart' and 'carbonado' are clusters of tiny crystals. Until diamonds are cut and polished, they do not sparkle like those you see on a ring – they just look like small, blue-grey stones.   10

In a rather crude form, the cutting and polishing of precious stones was an art known to the Ancient Egyptians, and in the Middle Ages it became widespread in north-west Europe. However, a revolutionary change in the methods of cutting and polishing was made in 1476 when Ludwig Van Berquen of Bruges in Belgium invented the use of a swiftly revolving   15 wheel with its edge faced with fine diamond powder. The name 'boart' is given to this fine powder as well as the natural crystalline material already mentioned. It is also given to badly flawed or broken diamond crystals, useless as jewels, that are broken into powder for grinding purposes, the so-called 'industrial' diamonds.   20

Diamond itself is the only material hard enough to cut and polish diamonds – though recently, high-intensity light beams called lasers have been developed which can bore holes in them. It may be necessary to split or cleave the large stones before they are cut and polished. Every diamond has a natural line of cleavage, along which it may be split by a   25 sharp blow with a cutting edge.

A fully cut 'brilliant' diamond has 58 facets, or faces, regularly arranged. For cutting or faceting, the stones are fixed into copper holders and held against a wheel, edged with a mixture of oil and fine diamond dust, which is revolved at about 2,500 revolutions a minute. Amsterdam and Antwerp,   30 in Holland and Belgium respectively, have been the centre of the diamond cutting and polishing industry for over seven centuries.

The jewel value of brilliant diamonds depends greatly on their colour, or 'water' as it is called. The usual colours of diamonds are white, yellow, brown, green, or blue-white; the blue-white brilliants are the stones of the   35 'finest water' and so command the highest prices. During their formation, some diamonds absorb metallic oxides from the surrounding rocks and take on their colour. Thus black, red and even bright pink diamonds have occasionally been found.

The trade in diamonds is not only in the valuable gem stones but also in   40
the industrial diamonds mentioned above. Zaire produces 70% of such
stones. They are fixed into the rock drills used in mining and civil
engineering, also for edging band saws for cutting stone. Diamond-faced
tools are used for cutting and drilling glass and fine porcelain, and for
dentists' drills. They are used as bearings in watches and other finely   45
balanced instruments. Perhaps you own some diamonds without knowing
it – in your wristwatch!

Ideas

Select the answer which is most accurate according to the information given
in the passage.

1   Since 1866
a)   most of the world's diamonds have come from Siberia.
b)   all the world's diamonds have come from near Kimberley in South
     Africa.
c)   Africa has produced nearly all the world's diamonds.
d)   diamonds have been discovered in most parts of the world.

2   'Carbonado' is the name given to
a)   only the very best diamonds.
b)   lumps of pure carbon.
c)   Spanish diamonds.
d)   diamonds made up of many small crystals.

3   After a diamond has been cut and polished, it
a)   looks like a small blue pebble.
b)   looks very different from its original form.
c)   can no longer be used to put in a ring.
d)   changes its chemical composition.

4   The art of cutting and polishing precious stones remained crude until
a)   the fourteenth century.
b)   the fifteenth century.
c)   the sixteenth century.
d)   the seventeenth century.

5   Industrial diamonds are
a)   made of a different substance from real diamonds.
b)   not as sparkling or brilliant as 'boart'.
c)   made up of diamond dust and broken crystals.
d)   produced artificially in factories.

6   During faceting, diamonds are held in copper holders
a)   to facilitate accurate cutting.
b)   to make them shine more brilliantly.
c)   so that they can revolve more easily.
d)   as a steel holder might damage the diamond.

Passage 6

7   The value order of 'water' in diamonds
a) is more important than their colour.
b) ranges from blue-white upwards.
c) ranges from blue-white downwards.
d) has never been reliably established.

8   Diamonds are
a) white, yellow, brown, green or blue-white.
b) all the same colour.
c) either blue or white in colour.
d) different colours depending on which rocks they come from.

9   Zaire produces
a) 70% of all diamonds sold.
b) 70% of industrial diamonds sold.
c) 70% of all precious stones sold.
d) 70% of the world's blue-white diamonds.

10 Industrial diamonds are used
a) for a wide range of purposes.
b) mainly for dentists' drills.
c) for decoration in rings and watches.
d) principally in mass-produced jewellery.

Vocabulary

Find the following words in the passage and select the meaning you think
is *most likely* to correspond among the choices given.

1   *crude* (line 11)
a) ill-mannered
b) uncultured
c) simple
d) uneducated

2   *faced* (line 16)
a) opposed
b) surfaced
c) confronted
d) decorated

3   *flawed* (line 18)
a) imperfectly formed
b) liquid
c) badly finished
d) dropped to the ground

4   *lasers* (line 22)
a) saws
b) energy beams
c) polishing machines
d) light planks of wood

5   *cleave* (line 24)
a) move
b) clip together
c) break
d) cut with sharp knife

6   *faceting* (line 28)
a) surface polishing
b) mounting
c) splitting
d) setting in rings

23

Passage 6

7 *command* (line 36)
a) order
b) bring
c) tell
d) instruct

8 *take on* (line 38)
a) adopt
b) continue
c) agree to do
d) fight

9 *fine* (line 44)
a) high quality
b) soft
c) sunny
d) payment

10 *bearings* (line 45)
a) directions
b) decorations
c) mechanical supports
d) straps

Missing word summary

Fill in the numbered blanks from the selection of words given below. The correct choices will complete the sense of this summary of the reading passage.

[1] diamonds have been found in India, Brazil and Siberia, most of them come from the African continent. Single large crystals of pure crystalline carbon are the most [2] kind, although they do not sparkle [3] they are cut and polished. The art of cutting and polishing diamonds has been known [4] the time of the Ancient Egyptians, but it was not until 1476, [5] the invention of Ludwig Van Berquen's [6] that the modern art of precision polishing developed. The colour or 'water' of a diamond [7] its value, though flawed diamonds are widely used in [8], as well as in delicate instruments such as watches.

1 a) Because
b) However
c) Although

2 a) common
b) valuable
c) colourful

3 a) until
b) after
c) although

4 a) before
b) since
c) along with

5 a) before
b) with
c) to

6 a) diamond dust
b) polishing wheel
c) 'boart' crystal

7 a) decides
b) reduces
c) increases

8 a) industry
b) jewellery
c) Zaire

24

Passage 7

Canning food

Food which is kept too long decays because it is attacked by yeasts, moulds
and bacteria. The canning process, however, seals the product in a container
so that no infection can reach it, and then it is sterilized by heat. Heat
sterilization destroys all infections present in food inside the can. No
chemical preservatives are necessary, and properly canned food does not   5
deteriorate during storage.

The principle was discovered in 1809 by a Frenchman called Nicolas
Appert. He corked food lightly in wide-necked *glass* bottles and immersed
them in a bath of hot water to drive out the air, then he hammered the
corks down to seal the jars hermetically. Appert's discovery was rewarded by   10
the French government because better preserved food supplies were needed
for Napoleon's troops on distant campaigns.

By 1814 an English manufacturer had replaced Appert's glass jars with
metal containers and was supplying tinned vegetable soup and meat to
the British navy. The next scientific improvement, in 1860, was the result   15
of Louis Pasteur's work on sterilization through the application of
scientifically controlled heat.

Today vegetables, fish, fruit, meat and beer are canned in enormous
quantities. Within three generations the eating habits of millions have been
revolutionized. Foods that were previously seasonal may now be eaten at   20
any time, and strange foods are available far from the countries where they
are grown. The profitable crops many farmers now produce often depend
on the proximity of a canning factory.

The first stage in the canning process is the preparation of the raw food.
Diseased and waste portions are thrown away; meat and fish are cleaned   25
and trimmed; fruit and vegetables washed and graded for size. The jobs are
principally done by machine.

The next stage, for vegetables only, is *blanching*. This is immersion in
very hot or boiling water for a short time to remove air and soften the
vegetable. This makes it easier to pack into cans for sterilization. Some   30
packing machines fill up to 400 cans a minute. Fruit, fish and meat are
packed raw and cold into cans, and then all the air is removed. When the
cans are sealed, the pressure inside each can is only about half the pressure
of the outside air. This is 'vacuum' packing.

During the sterilization process which follows, the cans are subjected to   35
steam or boiling water, with the temperature and duration varying according
to the type of food. Cans of fruit, for example, take only 5–10 minutes in
boiling water, while meat and fish are cooked at higher temperatures for

longer periods. After sterilization, the cans are cooled quickly to 32°C. to prevent the contents from becoming too soft.

The final stage before despatch to the wholesale or retail grocer is labelling, and packing the tins into boxes. Nowadays, however, labelling is often printed on in advance by the can-maker and no paper labels are then required.

40

Ideas

Say whether the following statements are true or false according to the information given in the passage.

1 Chemical preservatives are necessary in canned food.
2 Nicolas Appert, a Frenchman, was not the first man to preserve food in cans.
3 Food has been canned for two centuries now.
4 Napoleon rewarded Louis Pasteur for his work in the preservation of food.
5 Canning factories are often built close to the farms which supply them.
6 Much of the preparation of raw food for canning has to be done by hand.
7 *Blanching* is an essential step in all food canning.
8 Meat is cooked after it is packed in the cans.
9 The pressure inside vacuum-packed cans is about twice that of the outside air.
10 The sterilization process does not take more than 5–10 minutes.

Vocabulary

Find the following words in the passage and select the meaning you think is *most likely* to correspond among the choices given.

1 *decays* (line 1)
a) smells
b) waits
c) lasts a long time
d) goes bad

2 *seals* (line 2)
a) puts
b) closes up
c) packs
d) stores

3 *deteriorate* (line 6)
a) change for the worse
b) discourage
c) become soft
d) lose much moisture

4 *corks* (line 10)
a) kind of food
b) covers
c) nails
d) containers

5 *seasonal* (line 20)
a) peppery and spicy
b) rare and expensive
c) grown only at certain times
d) available only at irregular intervals

6 *proximity* (line 23)
a) nearness
b) rough estimate
c) approximate size
d) method

7 *raw* (line 32)
a) uncooked
b) neatly stacked
c) warm
d) whole

8 *vacuum* (line 34)
a) hygienic
b) low pressure
c) scientific
d) high pressure

9 *duration* (line 36)
a) hardness
b) durability
c) timing
d) pressure

10 *despatch* (line 41)
a) sending
b) message
c) dismissal
d) speed

Spot the topic

Which of the following choices a), b) or c) most adequately sums up the ideas of the *whole* paragraph?

1 *Para. 1* (lines 1–6)
a) Food scientifically sealed in cans is safe from decay.
b) Sterilization – the key to the safe-keeping of food.
c) The use of chemicals in preventing the decay of food.

2 *Paras. 2 and 3* (lines 7–17)
a) The history and early methods of preserving food.
b) The French influence in food canning.
c) The scientific principles of food canning.

3 *Para. 4* (lines 18–23)
a) How the canning industry affects our lives.
b) The economic effects of the canning industry.
c) The range and diverse advantages of canned food.

4 *Paras. 5–8* (lines 24–44)
a) The mechanical miracle of food canning.
b) The step-by-step modern processes of canning food.
c) The process of preparing, washing and grading food for canning.

5 *Paras. 5–8* (lines 24–44)
Put the following key processes in the order in which they occur. Number them 1–6.
a) blanching
b) preparing the raw food
c) labelling and packing
d) sterilizing
e) filling and sealing cans
f) cooling

The Olympic Games

In ancient Greece athletic festivals were very important and had strong
religious associations. The Olympian athletic festival, held every four years
in honour of Zeus, eventually lost its local character, became first a
national event, and then, after the rules against foreign competitors had
been waived, international. No one knows exactly how far back the   5
Olympic Games go, but some official records date from 776 B.C.

The Games took place in August on the plain by Mount Olympus. Many
thousands of spectators gathered from all parts of Greece, but no married
woman was admitted even as a spectator. Slaves, women and dishonoured
persons were not allowed to compete. The exact sequence of events is   10
uncertain, but events included boys' gymnastics, horse-racing, field events
such as discus and javelin throwing, and the very important foot races.
There was also boxing and wrestling and special tests of varied ability such
as the pentathlon, the winner of which excelled in running, jumping, discus
and javelin throwing and wrestling. The evening of the third day was   15
devoted to sacrificial offerings to the heroes of the day, and the fourth
day, that of the full moon, was set aside as a holy day.

On the sixth and last day, all the victors were crowned with holy
garlands of wild olive from a sacred wood. So great was the honour that
the winner of the foot race gave his name to the year of his victory.   20
Although Olympic winners received no prize money, they were, in fact,
richly rewarded by their state authorities. The public honour also made the
strict discipline of the ten-month training period worthwhile. In spite of the
lengthy training, however runners were known to drop dead from strain at
the winning post. How their results compared with modern standards,   25
we unfortunately have no means of telling.

After an uninterrupted history of almost 1,200 years, the Games were
abolished in A.D. 394, the Christian era, because of their pagan origin.
It was over 1,500 years before there was another such international
athletics gathering. The Greek institution was revived in 1896 and the   30
first small meeting took place in Athens. After the 1908 London Olympics,
success was re-established and nations sent their best representatives. In
times of peace, the Games have taken place ever since at four-yearly
intervals. In Munich in 1972, competitors from more than 120 countries
were watched by huge crowds.   35

Nowadays, the Games are held in different countries in turn. The host
country provides vast facilities, including a stadium, swimming pools and
living accommodation, but competing countries pay their own athletes'

expenses. Athletic contests are still the main feature, but now many more
sports are represented, women compete, the ancient pentathlon, for   40
example, has been modified into a more comprehensive test, and the
marathon* races, initiated in 1896, are now a celebrated event.

The Olympics start with the arrival in the stadium of a torch, lighted
on Mount Olympus by the sun's rays. It is carried by a succession of
runners to the stadium. The torch symbolizes the continuation of the   45
ancient Greek athletic ideals, and it burns throughout the Games until
the closing ceremony. The well-known Olympic flag, however, is a modern
conception: the five interlocking rings symbolize the uniting of all five
continents participating in the Games.

Ideas

Decide which answer best completes the following statements according
to the information in the passage.

1   The first Olympic Games took place
a)   in the seventh century A.D.
b)   certainly before 700 B.C.
c)   over three thousand years ago.
d)   a thousand years ago.

2   In the final stages of the ancient Olympic Games, any competitor had
     to be
a)   Greek.
b)   male.
c)   unmarried.
d)   neither a slave nor a foreigner.

3   The order of athletic events at the ancient Olympics
a)   has not definitely been established.
b)   varied according to the full moon.
ᵥc)   was decided by Zeus, in whose honour the Games were held.
d)   was considered unimportant.

4   During the Games, on the evening before the moon was full,
a)   heroes were sacrificed to Zeus.
b)   large sums of prize money were distributed to the heroes.
c)   all the victors were crowned with garlands.
d)   the heroes were honoured with sacrificial offerings.

5   Competitors had to train
a)   for four years.
b)   for ten months.
c)   until they collapsed exhausted.
d)   for periods determined by their state authorities.

* *marathon:* longest running race of all – about 42 kilometres (26 miles) in length.

6 Modern athletes' results cannot be compared with those of the ancient
   runners because
a) details such as times were not recorded in the past.
b) they are much better.
c) the ancient runners fell down dead.
d) the Greeks had no means of telling the time.

7 The continuity of the Olympic Games
a) was broken in the year A.D. 1200.
b) has never been broken.
c) was interrupted for over 1,500 years.
d) was broken in 1896.

8 Nowadays, the athletes' expenses are paid for
a) out of the national funds of competing nations.
b) out of the prize money of the winners.
c) by the athletes themselves.
d) by commercial organizations.

9 At the beginning of the Games in the host country
a) a torch is ignited at sunrise.
b) a lighted torch is brought into the stadium.
c) relays of runners light their torches in the stadium.
d) a torch is ignited by the Greek ambassador.

10 The modern Olympics compared with the ancient ones are
a) inspired by the same ideals.
b) completely different in every respect.
c) more restricted in the variety of events.
d) too much concerned with international rivalry.

Vocabulary

Find the following words in the passage and select the meaning you think
is *most likely* to correspond among the choices given.

1 *waived* (line 5)
a) accepted
b) shaken
c) abolished
d) displayed

2 *excelled in* (line 14)
a) was best overall at
b) chose between
c) was excessive in
d) was restricted to

3 *sacred* (line 19)
a) picturesque
b) of religious significance
c) frightened
d) carved with a knife

4 *rewarded* (line 22)
a) paid
b) prized
c) gifted
d) valued

5   *pagan* (line 28)
a) evil
b) irreligious
c) heathen
d) pageant-like

8   *initiated* (line 42)
a) run
b) continued
c) begun
d) accepted into adulthood

6   *institution* (line 30)
a) museum
b) custom
c) school
d) building

9   *conception* (line 48)
a) birth
b) beginning
c) idea
d) instrument

7   *facilities* (line 37)
a) opportunities
b) buildings and equipment
c) entertainments
d) faculties

10 *interlocking* (line 48)
a) linked
b) international
c) doubled
d) touching

Similar or different?

Say whether or not the statement is similar in meaning to the sentence from the passage indicated by the line number in brackets.

1   We can ascertain when the Olympic Games first took place because official records date from 776 B.C. (lines 5–6)
2   Originally the only permitted competitors were those whose position in society was respected. (lines 9–10)
3   Because the ten-month period of training was so strenuous, competitors who did not achieve success felt that their efforts were wasted. (lines 22–23)
4   The intensive training gave all runners the strength to withstand even the strain of the great races. (lines 23–25)
5   As there is a greater variety of sports nowadays, athletic events have lost their importance. (lines 39–40)
6   The Olympic torch burns throughout the Games to honour today the ancient Greek athletic ideals. (lines 45–46)

Passage 9

Auction sales

Auctions are public sales of goods, conducted by an officially approved auctioneer. He asks the crowd assembled in the auction-room to make offers, or 'bids', for the various items on sale. He encourages buyers to bid higher figures, and finally names the highest bidder as the buyer of the goods. This is called 'knocking down' the goods, for the bidding ends when 5 the auctioneer bangs a small hammer on a table at which he stands. This is often set on a raised platform called a rostrum.

The ancient Romans probably invented sales by auction, and the English word comes from the Latin *auctio*, meaning 'increase'. The Romans usually sold in this way the spoils taken in war; these sales were called 10 *sub hasta,* meaning 'under the spear', a spear being stuck in the ground as a signal for a crowd to gather. In England in the eighteenth and nineteenth centuries goods were often sold 'by the candle': a short candle was lit by the auctioneer, and bids could be made while it stayed alight.

Practically all goods whose qualities vary are sold by auction. Among 15 these are coffee, hides, skins, wool, tea, cocoa, furs, spices, fruit and vegetables and wines. Auction sales are also usual for land and property, antique furniture, pictures, rare books, old china and similar works of art. The auction-rooms at Christie's and Sotheby's in London and New York are world-famous. 20

An auction is usually advertised beforehand with full particulars of the articles to be sold and where and when they can be viewed by prospective buyers. If the advertisement cannot give full details, catalogues are printed, and each group of goods to be sold together, called a 'lot', is usually given a number. The auctioneer need not begin with Lot 1 and continue in 25 numerical order; he may wait until he registers the fact that certain dealers are in the room and then produce the lots they are likely to be interested in. The auctioneer's services are paid for in the form of a percentage of the price the goods are sold for. The auctioneer therefore has a direct interest in pushing up the bidding as high as possible. 30

The auctioneer must know fairly accurately the current market values of the goods he is selling, and he should be acquainted with regular buyers of such goods. He will not waste time by starting the bidding too low. He will also play on the rivalries among his buyers and succeed in getting a high price by encouraging two business competitors to bid against each 35 other. It is largely on his advice that a seller will fix a 'reserve' price, that is, a price below which the goods cannot be sold. Even the best auctioneers, however, find it difficult to stop a 'knock-out', whereby dealers illegally

arrange beforehand not to bid against each other, but nominate one of
themselves as the only bidder, in the hope of buying goods at extremely   40
low prices. If such a 'knock-out' comes off, the real auction sale takes
place privately afterwards among the dealers.

Ideas

Select the answer which is most accurate according to the information
given in the passage.

1   Auctioned goods are sold
a) for the highest price offered.
b) only at fixed prices.
c) at a price less than their true value.
d) very cheaply.

2   The end of the bidding is called 'knocking down' because
a) the auctioneer knocks the buyer down.
b) the auctioneer knocks the rostrum down.
c) the goods are knocked down on to the table.
d) the auctioneer bangs the table with a hammer.

3   The Romans used to sell by auction
a) spoilt goods.
b) old worn-out weapons.
c) property taken from the enemy.
d) spears.

4   A candle used to burn at auction sales
a) because they took place at night.
b) as a signal for the crowd to gather.
c) to keep the auctioneer warm.
d) to limit the time when offers could be made.

5   An auction catalogue gives prospective buyers
a) the current market values of the goods.
b) details of the goods to be sold.
c) the order in which goods must be sold.
d) free admission to the auction sale.

6   The auctioneer may decide to sell the 'lots' out of order because
a) he sometimes wants to confuse the buyers.
b) he knows from experience that certain people will want to buy certain
    items.
c) he wants to keep certain people waiting.
d) he wants to reduce the number of buyers.

Passage 9

7   An auctioneer likes to get high prices for the goods he sells because
a)   then he earns more himself.
b)   the dealers are pleased.
c)   the auction-rooms become world-famous.
d)   it keeps the customers interested.

8   A clever auctioneer encourages
a)   knock-out deals.
b)   rivals to compete in high bidding.
c)   the seller to accept the lowest price offered.
d)   dealers to buy from each other.

9   'Knock-outs' are illegal agreements
a)   between auctioneers and dealers.
b)   between the seller and the auctioneer.
c)   among the dealers only.
d)   among the sellers only.

10 A 'knock-out' is arranged
a)   to keep the price in the auction-room low.
b)   to allow one dealer only to make a profit.
c)   to increase the auctioneer's profit.
d)   to help the auctioneer.

Vocabulary

Find the following words in the passage and select the meaning you think
is *most likely* to correspond among the choices given.

1   *bidder* (line 4)
a)   one who buys
b)   one who sells
c)   auctioneer
d)   one who makes an offer

2   *to gather* (line 12)
a)   to collect
b)   together
c)   to pick
d)   to understand

3   *particulars* (line 21)
a)   details
b)   special
c)   parts
d)   prices

4   *prospective* (line 22)
a)   ambitious
b)   intending
c)   fortune-hunting
d)   uninterested

5   *numerical* (line 26)
a)   numerous
b)   random
c)   as numbered on a list
d)   rapid

6   *registers* (line 26)
a)   notices
b)   writes down
c)   authorizes
d)   changes

7   *percentage* (line 28)
a) one-hundredth
b) proportion
c) 10%
d) half

8   *pushing up* (line 30)
a) raising
b) rising
c) growing
d) exceeding

9   *current* (line 31)
a) electrical
b) up-to-date
c) useful
d) flowing

10   *comes off* (line 41)
a) goes wrong
b) is successful
c) is taken away
d) can be removed

Missing word summary

Fill in the numbered blanks from the selection of words given below. The correct choices will complete the sense of this summary of the reading passage.

An auction is a [1] of goods. The auctioneer asks the crowd gathered to make [2]. The [3] bidder is the person who eventually buys the goods. Among products sold [4] auction are coffee, furs and wine as well as property, furniture and works of art. The auctioneer urges the bidding as high as possible [5] he [6] a percentage of the price obtained. He knows the dealers but cannot prevent a group of them [7] in a 'knock-out'.

1   a) sell
    b) sale
    c) dealer

2   a) bidders
    b) bids
    c) goods

3   a) first
    b) loudest
    c) highest

4   a) by
    b) in
    c) at

5   a) because
    b) although
    c) so that

6   a) has paid
    b) is paying
    c) is paid

7   a) to unite
    b) from uniting
    c) to have

The planemakers

There are two main things that make aircraft engineering difficult: the
need to make every component as reliable as possible and the need to
build everything as light as possible. The fact that an aeroplane is up in
the air and cannot stop if anything goes wrong, makes it perhaps a matter
of life or death that its performance is absolutely dependable.   5

Given a certain power of engine, and consequently a certain fuel consumption, there is a practical limit to the total weight of aircraft that can
be made to fly. Out of that weight as much as possible is wanted for fuel,
radio navigational instruments, passenger seats, or freight room, and, of
course, the passengers or freight themselves. So the structure of the aircraft   10
has to be as small and light as safety and efficiency will allow. The
designer must calculate the normal load that each part will bear. This
specialist is called the 'stress man'. He takes account of any unusual stress
that may be put on the part as a precaution against errors in manufacture,
accidental damage, etc.   15

The stress man's calculations go to the designer of the part, and he must
make it as strong as the stress man says is necessary. One or two samples
are always tested to prove that they are as strong as the designer intended.
Each separate part is tested, then a whole assembly – for example, a
complete wing, and finally the whole aeroplane. When a new type of   20
aeroplane is being made, normally only one of the first three made will
be flown. Two will be destroyed on the ground in structural tests. The
third one will be tested in the air.

Two kinds of ground strength tests are carried out. The first is to find
the resistance to loading of the wings, tail, etc. until they reach their   25
maximum load and collapse. The other test is for fatigue strength.
Relatively small loads are applied thousands of times. Each may be well
under what the structure could stand as a single load, but many repetitions
can result in collapse. One form of this test is done on the passenger cabin.
It is filled with air at high pressure as for high-altitude flying and completely 30
submerged in a large tank of water while the test is going on. The surrounding
water prevents the cabin from bursting like a bomb if there is a failure.

When a plane has passed all the tests it can get a government certificate
of airworthiness, without which it is illegal to fly, except for test flying.

Making the working parts reliable is as difficult as making the structure   35
strong enough. The flying controls, the electrical equipment, the fire
precautions, etc. must not only be light in weight, but must work both at
high altitudes where the temperature may be below freezing point and in
the hot air of an airfield in the tropics.

36

Passage 10

To solve all these problems the aircraft industry has a large number of   40
research workers, with elaborate laboratories and test houses, and new
materials to give the best strength in relation to weight are constantly
being tested.

Ideas

Select the answer which is most accurate according to the information
given in the passage.

1   The two main requirements of aircraft design are
a)   speed and cheapness.
b)   reliability and passenger comfort.
c)   making things both light and dependable.
d)   ability to stay up in the air and avoid breakdowns.

2   The maximum possible weight of an aircraft is determined by
a)   the engine power.
b)   the amount of freight room.
c)   the number of passengers.
d)   international regulations.

3   The stress man's job is to calculate
a)   how safe the plane is.
b)   how strong each part must be.
c)   what height the plane will fly at.
d)   the amount of luggage each passenger may carry.

4   The first three aeroplanes of a new type
a)   are all destroyed.
b)   do not fly.
c)   are later broken up for spare parts.
d)   are used for testing purposes.

5   The passenger cabin test in water is designed to
a)   make sure the plane would be safe if it landed in water.
b)   test fatigue strength.
c)   see if the cabin will burst like a bomb.
d)   keep the cabin cool

6   All equipment in an aircraft must
a)   work especially well at high temperatures.
b)   be tested to destruction.
c)   not be too light in weight.
d)   work perfectly within a wide range of temperatures.

7   Certificates of airworthiness are issued by
a)   the aircraft industry.
b)   research workers.
c)   stress men.
d)   governments.

8   Research workers
a)   are employed in large numbers by the aircraft industry.
b)   seldom find solutions to practical problems.
c)   also test houses.
d)   do not need elaborate laboratories.

9   New materials are
a)   too expensive to use in aircraft.
b)   avoided if possible.
c)   put to a variety of tests.
d)   tested at a constant temperature.

10 Except for experimental flights, no new aircraft leaves the ground
a)   after being completely tested for safety.
b)   without having a stress man on board.
c)   until it has been thoroughly tested and approved.
d)   unless flown by a government official.

Vocabulary

Find the following words in the passage and select the meaning you think
is *most likely* to correspond among the choices given.

1   *component* (line 2)
a)   complete
b)   employee
c)   part
d)   engineer

2   *performance* (line 5)
a)   show
b)   operation
c)   appearance
d)   demonstration

3   *navigational* (line 9)
a)   steering
b)   navy
c)   shipping
d)   recreational

4   *freight* (line 10)
a)   cargo
b)   fear
c)   free
d)   cooking

5   *efficiency* (line 11)
a)   regular servicing
b)   adequate precautions
c)   effective operation
d)   speed

6   *precaution* (line 14)
a)   warning bell
b)   safety measure
c)   complaint
d)   protest

7   *fatigue strength* (line 26)
a)   inability to resist tiredness
b)   strong feeling of tiredness
c)   prolonged resistance to weakening
d)   tendency to become weary

8   *relatively* (line 27)
a)   comparatively
b)   connectedly
c)   excessively
d)   connected

9   *submerged* (line 31)
a)   overburdened
b)   suppressed
c)   put below the surface
d)   raised

10   *elaborate* (line 41)
a)   expensively jewelled
b)   difficult
c)   complicated
d)   decorated

Similar or different?

Say whether or not the statement is similar in meaning to the sentence from the passage indicated by the line number in brackets.

1   An aircraft has to operate as perfectly as possible because people might die if anything went wrong while it was in flight. (lines 3–5)
2   The total possible weight of an aircraft depends on the power of the engine and the amount of fuel it requires. (lines 6–8)
3   Two tests are made on the strength of the ground. (line 24)
4   Repeating the loading many times may cause a part to break up even though each single load is within the limits of safety. (lines 27–29)
5   Making the structure strong enough is no less difficult than making the working parts dependable. (lines 35–36)
6   It is not an essential for the controls, the equipment, the safety measures to be light-weight, but they must work efficiently within a wide range of temperatures. (lines 36–39)

Dreams – what do they mean?

Dreams have always held a universal fascination. Some primitive societies
believe that the soul leaves the body and visits the scene of the dream.
Generally, however, dreams are accepted to be illusions, having much in
common with day-dreams – the fantasies of our waking life. When dreaming,
however, one tends to believe fully in the reality of the dream world,   5
however inconsistent, illogical and odd it may be.

Although most dreams apparently happen spontaneously, dream activity
may be provoked by external influences. 'Suffocation' dreams are connected
with the breathing difficulties of a heavy cold, for instance. Internal
disorders such as indigestion can cause vivid dreams, and dreams of racing   10
fire-engines may be caused by the ringing of an alarm bell.

Experiments have been carried out to investigate the connection between
deliberately inflicted pain and dreaming. For example, a sleeper pricked with
a pin perhaps dreams of fighting a battle and receiving a severe sword wound.
Although the dream is stimulated by the physical discomfort, the actual   15
events of the dream depend on the associations of the discomfort in the
mind of the sleeper.

A dreamer's eyes often move rapidly from side to side. Since people
born blind do not dream visually and do not manifest this eye activity, it
is thought that the dreamer may be scanning the scene depicted in his   20
dream. A certain amount of dreaming seems to be a human requirement
– if a sleeper is roused every time his eyes begin to move fast, effectively
depriving him of his dreams, he will make more eye movements the
following night.

People differ greatly in their claims to dreaming. Some say they dream   25
every night, others only very occasionally. Individual differences probably
exist, but some people immediately forget dreams and others have good
recall.

Superstition and magical practices thrive on the supposed power of
dreams to foretell the future. Instances of dreams which have later turned   30
out to be prophetic have often been recorded, some by men of the
highest intellectual integrity. Although it is better to keep an open mind
on the subject, it is true that the alleged power of dreams to predict future
events still remains unproved.

Everyone knows that a sleeping dog often behaves as though he were   35
dreaming, but it is impossible to tell what his whines and twitches really
mean. By analogy with human experience, however, it is reasonable to
suppose that at least the higher animals are capable of dreaming.

Of the many theories of dreams, Freud's is probably the best known.

According to Freud, we revert in our dreams to the modes of thought 40
characteristic of early childhood. Our thinking becomes concrete,
pictorial and non-logical, and expresses ideas and wishes we are no longer
conscious of. Dreams are absurd and unaccountable because our conscious
mind, not willing to acknowledge our subconscious ideas, disguises them.
Some of Freud's interpretations are extremely fanciful, but there is almost 45
certainly some truth in his view that dreams express the subconscious
mind.

Ideas

Say whether the following statements are true or false according to the
information given in the passage.

1 Dreams while we are asleep are quite different from day-dreams.
2 Dreams may be caused by an upset stomach.
3 If you prick someone with a pin, he may dream he has been stabbed.
4 Sighted people and those who have never been able to see dream in
  exactly the same way.
5 Dreaming is probably unnecessary.
6 There is plenty of proof available that dreams foretell the future.
7 Everyone knows that dogs dream just like human beings.
8 Because human beings dream, so may the more intelligent animals.
9 Dreams are not easy to interpret because the original thoughts and
  ideas are disguised.
10 It is almost certainly true that dreams express the subconscious mind.

Vocabulary

Find the following words in the passage and select the meaning you think
is *most likely* to correspond among the choices given.

1 *inconsistent* (line 6)
a) contained
b) contradictory
c) discontented
d) unconscious

2 *spontaneously* (line 7)
a) without apparent cause
b) frequently
c) at night
d) without notes

3 *suffocation* (line 8)
a) choking
b) breathing
c) suffering
d) cutting off

4 *deliberately* (line 13)
a) freely
b) cruelly
c) intentionally
d) considerately

5 *effectively* (line 22)
a) usefully
b) actually
c) for his own good
d) economically

6 *thrive* (line 29)
a) three times
b) flourish
c) disbelieve
d) try

7 *instances* (line 30)
a) parts
b) moments
c) examples
d) accidents

8 *alleged* (line 33)
a) claimed to be true
b) well known to be true
c) true
d) legal

9 *unaccountable* (line 43)
a) unregistered
b) unpaid for ,
c) not reasonable
d) not possible to record

10 *acknowledge* (line 44)
a) recognize
b) suppress
c) teach others
d) cover up

Spot the topic

Which of the following choices a), b) or c) most adequately sums up the ideas of the *whole* paragraph?

1 *Para. 1* (lines 1–6)
a) Fantastic dreams.
b) Attitudes to dreams.
c) The dream world.

2 *Para. 2* (lines 7–11)
a) Probable causes of dreams.
b) The effects of dreams.
c) The vividness of dreams.

3 *Para. 3* (lines 12–17)
a) Science and dream sequences.
b) How the mind conditions dreams.
c) How pain may affect dreams.

4 *Para. 4* (lines 18–24)
a) Eye-movement in dreams – its possible significance.
b) The difference between dreaming in the sighted and the blind.
c) The apparent need for humans to dream.

5 *Para. 6* (lines 29–34)
a) Beliefs about dreaming.
b) Are dreams prophetic?
c) Dreams foretell the future.

6 *Para. 8* (lines 39–47)
a) Freud's dreams.
b) Freud and the dreams of early childhood.
c) The Freudian interpretation of dreaming.

Passage 12

To be or not to be a vegetarian

A strict vegetarian is a person who never in his life eats anything derived
from animals. The main objection to vegetarianism on a long-term basis
is the difficulty of getting enough protein – the body-building element
in food. If you have ever been without meat or other animal foods for
some days of weeks (say, for religious reasons) you will have noticed that   5
you tend to get physically rather weak. You are glad when the fast is over
and you get your reward of a succulent meat meal.

Proteins are built up from approximately twenty food elements called
'amino-acids', which are found more abundantly in animal protein than in
vegetable protein. This means you have to eat a great deal more vegetable   10
than animal food in order to get enough of these amino-acids. A great deal
of the vegetable food goes to waste in this process and from the physiological point of view there is not much to be said in favour of life-long
vegetarianism.

The economic side of the question, though, must be considered. Vege-   15
table food is much cheaper than animal food. However, since only a small
proportion of the vegetable protein is useful for body-building purposes, a
consistent vegetarian, if he is to gain the necessary 70 grams of protein a
day, has to consume a greater bulk of food than his digestive organs can
comfortably deal with. In fairness, though, it must be pointed out that   20
vegetarians *claim* they need far less than 70 grams of protein a day.

Whether or not vegetarianism should be advocated for adults, it is
definitely unsatisfactory for growing children, who need more protein
than they can get from vegetable sources. A lacto-vegetarian diet, which
includes milk and milk products such as cheese, can, however, be satis-   25
factory as long as enough milk and milk products are consumed.

Meat and cheese are the best sources of usable animal protein and next
come milk, fish and eggs.

Slow and careful cooking of meat makes it more digestible and assists
in the breaking down of the protein content by the body. When cooking   30
vegetables, however, the vitamins, and in particular the water-soluble
vitamin C, should not be lost through over-cooking.

With fruit, vitamin loss is negligible, because the cooking water is
normally eaten along with the fruit, and acids in the fruit help to hold in
the vitamin C.   35

Most nutrition experts today would recommend a balanced diet containing elements of all foods, largely because of our need for sufficient
vitamins. Vitamins were first called 'accessory food factors' since it was

43

discovered, in 1906, that most foods contain, besides carbohydrates, fats, minerals and water, these other substances necessary for health. The most common deficiencies in Western diets today are those of vitamins. The answer is variety in food. A well-balanced diet having sufficient amounts of milk, fruit, vegetables, eggs, and meat, fish or fowl (i.e. any good protein source) usually provides adequate minimum daily requirements of all the vitamins.

40

45

Ideas

Select the answer which is most accurate according to the information given in the passage.

1   A strict vegetarian
a)   rarely eats animal products.
b)   sometimes eats eggs.
c)   never eats any animal products.
d)   never eats protein.

2   We feel weak when we go without meat and other animal products
a)   because we are reducing our food intake.
b)   because we do not get enough protein.
c)   because vegetables do not contain protein.
d)   unless we take plenty of exercise.

3   Proteins are built up from
a)   approximately twenty different foods.
b)   about twenty different vegetables.
c)   various fats and sugars.
d)   about twenty different amino-acids.

4   Physiologically, life-long vegetarianism may not be good because
a)   it makes people very thin.
b)   the body must process too much waste.
c)   the farmers lose money.
d)   vitamin-deficiency diseases may result.

5   One thing in favour of vegetarianism is that
a)   vegetable food is easier to digest.
b)   animal food is less expensive.
c)   vegetable food is cheaper.
d)   it is good for the digestion.

6   The body's daily need for protein is
a)   90 grams.
b)   50 grams.
c)   70 grams.
d)   at least 100 grams.

7   The digestive organs can comfortably deal with
a)   any quantity of food per day.
b)   less than 70 grams of food per day.
c)   a limited quantity of food per day.
d)   any amount of vegetable foods.

8   Vegetarianism is not suitable for growing children because they
a)   need more protein than vegetables can supply.
b)   cannot digest vegetables.
c)   use more energy than adults.
d)   cannot easily digest milk and milk products.

9   Slow and careful cooking of meat
a)   preserves the vitamins.
b)   breaks down the vitamins.
c)   makes it easier to digest.
d)   reduces the protein content.

10 Most nutrition experts today believe the food we eat should contain
a)   more meat than vegetables.
b)   more vegetables than meat.
c)   fruit, cereals and fish as well as meat and vegetables.
d)   as many different kinds of vegetables as possible.

Vocabulary

Find the following words in the passage and select the meaning you think
is *most likely* to correspond among the choices given.

1   *strict* (line 1)
a)   fierce
b)   complete
c)   harsh
d)   cruel

2   *rather* (line 6)
a)   preferably
b)   hardly
c)   better
d)   somewhat

3   *succulent* (line 7)
a)   tasty
b)   soft
c)   small
d)   sucking

4   *abundantly* (line 9)
a)   excessively
b)   occasionally
c)   plentifully
d)   rarely

5   *physiological* (line 13)
a)   bodily
b)   mental
c)   psychological
d)   medicinal

6   *consistent* (line 18)
a)   content
b)   hard-working
c)   regular
d)   agreeable

7	*advocated* (line 22)	9	*consumed* (line 26)
a)	discussed	a)	used up
b)	recommended	b)	eaten
c)	disputed	c)	destroyed
d)	made legal	d)	completed

8	*lacto-vegetarian* (line 24)	10	*in particular* (line 31)
a)	milk and meat	a)	with care
b)	partly meat	b)	in part
c)	part milk, part vegetable	c)	especially
d)	non-protein	d)	in detail

Missing word summary

Fill in the numbered blanks from the selection of words given below. The correct choices will complete the sense of this summary of the reading passage.

A strict vegetarian is a person who [1] himself of any animal product. The danger of [2] this is that one may [3] get enough protein. Vegetables [4] contain protein, however, and vegetarians claim that they need [5] than the 70 grams per day that some dieticians suggest [6]. Growing children definitely need milk and milk products, so a [7] diet is the only satisfactory form of [8] for them.

1	a) prevents b) deprives c) allows	5	a) far more b) far less c) not less
2	a) making b) doing c) having	6	a) necessarily b) necessity c) necessary
3	a) no b) not c) perhaps	7	a) strict vegetarian b) non-vegetarian c) lacto-vegetarian
4	a) do b) do not c) seldom	8	a) vegetable b) vegetarian c) vegetarianism

Passage 13

Making leather

Hides and skins are the raw material of the leather manufacturer or tanner. When man first used animal skins is not known. Skins, even when preserved by tanning, do not last as long as stone, pottery, metals and bone, and our knowledge about the early use of skins is vague. However, the numerous flint scrapers and bone or ivory sewing needles in our museums show that   5 tens of thousands of years ago, in the early Stone Age, skins were prepared and used long before textiles. Nowadays, hides and skins are essential raw materials and important articles of commerce.

Any animal skin can be made into leather, but the skins chiefly used come from cattle, sheep, goats, pigs and horses. To a lesser extent the skins   10 from dogs, deer, reptiles, marine animals, fish and birds are also used. Snakes, lizards, seals, whales, and sharks all contribute to leather manufacture.

'Hide' is the trade word for the skins of the larger animals such as full-grown cattle and horses; and 'skin' for the smaller animals, and immature   15 large animals such as ponies and calves. Some skins are made into leather after the hair or wool has been removed; but the skins of the fur-bearing animals and sometimes of sheep, lambs and ponies are processed, or 'dressed', with the hair or wool still in place.

Most cattle hides come from South America, the U.S.A. and from   20 Australia with smaller quantities from East and West Africa, Central America and the Sudan. Sheepskins come from Australia and New Zealand, and the best goat skins come from India, Pakistan, Ethiopia, Arabia and Nigeria.

There is usually a long interval between the flaying, or stripping, of   25 the skin from the animal and putting it into the tannery for processing. If the flayed skins were left wet, they would go bad, just like meat; they must therefore be preserved in some way. The commonest method is salting. This involves sprinkling the skins with salt on their inner side; or immersing the skins completely in strong salt solution for some hours,   30 after which they are drained and sprinkled with solid salt.

Another method of drying is to stretch the skins out on the ground, or on frames and to dry them in the sun, or even better in the shade. Beetles and other insects eat skins and must be kept away by the use of some chemical such as D.D.T. The dried skins are called 'crust' leather   35 and are sent in this form to the tanneries for the very complicated process of tanning. After tanning, only the 'corium' or middle layer of the skin is left to provide leather as we know it. It is to the closely knit fibre structure

of the corium that leather owes its virtues of flexibility, strength and
elasticity, its resistance to rubbing and its unique power of allowing water   40
vapour and air to pass through it while resisting penetration by liquid water
itself.

Ideas

Select the answer which is most accurate according to the information given
in the passage.

1   Skins do not last as long as pottery
a) unless they are preserved by tanning.
b) however well preserved by tanning.
c) except after certain processes.
d) unless made into leather.

2   Our knowledge about the early use of skins is vague
a) because there is no evidence.
b) even though there is some evidence in the form of tools.
c) although numerous Stone Age skins have survived.
d) in spite of some written evidence.

3   Textiles started to be made
a) long before skins.
b) at about the same time as skins.
c) long after skins started to be used.
d) long before stone tools.

4   Leather can be made from the skins of
a) any animals except fish and birds.
b) any kind of animal.
c) cattle, sheep, goats, pigs and horses only.
d) the larger animals only.

5   The skins of sheep, lambs and ponies are dressed
a) with the hair or wool still in place.
b) in one of two different ways.
c) after the hair or wool has been removed.
d) with the hair or wool added later.

6   The difference between a hide and a skin
a) has never been defined.
b) depends on the type of tanning process.
c) is largely a question of size.
d) varies from country to country.

7   Cattle hides come mainly from
a) Africa.
b) The Americas and Australia.

Passage 13

c) the Sudan.
d) Australia and New Zealand.

8 Skins are usually preserved with salt after stripping
a) because they cannot be tanned immediately.
b) to preserve their moisture.
c) to make them taste better.
d) to keep insects away.

9 Unless specially treated, sun-dried skins may be attacked by
a) beetles.
b) white arsenic.
c) D.D.T.
d) various chemicals.

10 When the 'crust' leather has been processed by tanning
a) the 'corium' is discarded.
b) the 'corium' forms the middle layer.
c) nothing but the 'corium' remains.
d) it becomes airtight and waterproof.

Vocabulary

Find the following words in the passage and select the meaning you think
is *most likely* to correspond among the choices given.

1 *tanner* (line 1)
a) raw material supplier
b) hunter
c) skin manufacturer
d) leather processor

2 *flint scrapers* (line 5)
a) tools for scraping stone
b) tools for scraping flint
c) men who prepare hides and skins.
d) tools for preparing leather

3 *prepared* (line 6)
a) processed
b) ready
c) eaten
d) cooked

4 *immature* (line 15)
a) not fully grown
b) unripe
c) badly shaped
d) too young to be used

5 *dressed* (line 19)
a) clothed
b) made into cloth
c) tanned
d) put on

6 *flaying* (line 25)
a) peeling
b) hitting
c) whipping
d) preserving

7 *commonest* (line 28)
a) most usual
b) cheapest
c) simplest
d) quickest

8 *sprinkling* (line 29)
a) beating
b) stretching
c) covering lightly
d) rolling

49

9 *immersing* (line 30)
a) washing clean
b) drying
c) soaking
d) dipping briefly

10 *virtues* (line 39)
a) qualities
b) morals
c) disadvantages
d) purity

Similar or different?

Say whether or not the statement is similar in meaning to the sentence from the passage indicated by the line number in brackets.

1 Indications of the early use of skins by man are the tools used to prepare and sew them. (lines 5–7)
2 Some skins can be made into leather before or after the hair or wool has been removed. (lines 16–19)
3 Unless skins are left moist, like meat, they decay. (line 27)
4 Each skin must go through 4 processes: (*a*) salt is sprinkled on the inside; (*b*) it is immersed in a salt solution; (*c*) it is drained; (*d*) it is resprinkled with dry salt. (lines 29–31)
5 It is preferable to dry skins quickly rather than in the shade. (lines 32–33)
6 After the skins have dried into 'crust' leather, there is very little else to do. (lines 35–37)

Passage 14

Cats

The cat has probably been associated with Man since it was first given a
place by his fire in return for keeping the cave dwelling free of rats and
mice. The relationship between the cat and Man has not been constant,
however. Man's attitude has ranged through indifference and neglect to
the extremes of persecution and worship.   5

To the early Egyptians, the cat was a goddess and temples were built
in her honour. Probably the most revered of animal deities was Bast, the
cat-headed goddess. There was even a city, Bubastis, named after her.
Occasionally, Bast was depicted as lion-headed, but the majority of the
statues of her show her as cat-headed, often surrounded by sacred cats   10
or kittens.

The Egyptians had great faith in the power of a living cat to protect
them from both natural and supernatural evils. They made small ornaments
and charms representing cats and the various cat deities. These decorated
their homes and were buried with them to ensure that the soul of the   15
dead person was protected on its perilous journey through the hostile
spirit world.

Pious Egyptians always mummified* their cats and had them buried with
almost as much reverence as if they were human beings. At the end of the
last century, a cat cemetery was discovered near the site of the ancient   20
city of Bubastis. Here literally hundreds of thousands of little cat mummies
were found ranged neatly on shelves. Some were stolen, some destroyed,
and antique dealers sold many to tourists. Thousands were left.

An Alexandrian speculator finally thought of a way of turning them
into money. He offered them for sale as manure and, in 1890 he had a   25
cargo of 180,000 of them shipped to Liverpool. They were sold by auction
and the auctioneer actually used one instead of his hammer! They made
less than £4 *a ton*, much less than the value of a single specimen today.

The ancient Jews believed that when a religious person who had reached
a high degree of sanctity died, his soul entered the body of a cat and   30
remained there until the cat itself died a natural death. Only then could
it enter Paradise.

Exactly the same belief existed in Burma and Thailand until comparatively recently, and beautiful sacred cats were kept in great luxury in the
temples. When a member of the royal house of Siam died, his favourite   35
cat was buried alive with him but a small opening was always left for its

* *mummify:* preserve by embalming with chemicals. Ancient Egyptian bodies of men or animals
preserved in this way are called 'mummies'.

escape. When the cat emerged, the priests knew that the Prince's soul had safely entered its feline host, and the cat was ceremonially escorted to the Temple. At the crowning of the young King of Siam in 1926, a white cat was carried by a court official in the procession to the Throne Room. The   40
old King's soul was resting in this cat, and his faithful former courtiers knew that he would want to be present at the crowning of his successor.

Ideas

Select the answer which is most accurate according to the information given in the passage.

1   Man's attitude towards cats has
a)   always been friendly.
b)   been constant through the ages.
c)   always gone to extremes.
d)   been through many changes.

2   Bubastis was
a)   an Egyptian cat.
b)   an Egyptian city.
c)   an Egyptian goddess.
d)   usually depicted as cat-headed.

3   The ancient Egyptians believed cats
a)   protected them from natural and supernatural evils.
b)   could not affect life in the spirit world.
c)   attacked the souls of the dead in the spirit world.
d)   contained the souls of dead people.

4   In ancient Egypt cats were
a)   cremated after death.
b)   preserved after their death.
c)   buried alive.
d)   decorated with ornaments and charms.

5   The cat mummies in the cemetery at Bubastis numbered
a)   180,000.
b)   1,890.
c)   hundreds of thousands.
d)   millions.

6   At the end of the nineteenth century, thousands of mummified cats were
a)   sold as manure.
b)   used instead of hammers.
c)   re-buried in Liverpool, England.
d)   discovered at Alexandria.

7   A cat mummy would now
a)   be worth much more than £4.
b)   weigh a ton.
c)   not be worth anything.
d)   be quite a commonplace possession.

8   The ancient Jews believed
a)   a good man's soul was protected by a cat in the underworld.
b)   a cat's soul entered a good person's body.
c)   a good person's soul entered a cat.
d)   a cat would live only with holy people.

9   In Burma and Thailand people shared a belief about cats with
a)   the ancient Egyptians.
b)   the ancient Jews.
c)   the ancient Greeks.
d)   most of the civilized world.

10 At the 1926 Coronation a white cat was
a)   crowned the King of Siam.
b)   believed to be the spiritual guardian of the old king.
c)   cruelly buried while still alive.
d)   given to the new king as a present.

Vocabulary

Find the following words in the passage and select the meaning you think
is *most likely* to correspond among the choices given.

1   *indifference* (line 4)
a)   sameness
b)   similarity
c)   hatred
d)   not caring

2   *persecution* (line 5)
a)   cruel treatment
b)   adoration
c)   capital punishment
d)   mild dislike

3   *perilous* (line 16)
a)   long
b)   dangerous
c)   dark
d)   slow

4   *speculator* (line 24)
a)   business man
b)   spectator
c)   short-sighted man
d)   magician

5   *specimen* (line 28)
a)   species
b)   speciality
c)   example
d)   experiment

6   *sanctity* (line 30)
a)   old age
b)   wisdom
c)   sickness
d)   holiness

7 *comparatively* (line 33)
a) less
b) more
c) fairly
d) very

8 *feline* (line 38)
a) cat
b) large
c) painful
d) male

9 *escorted* (line 38)
a) accompanied
b) honoured
c) escaped
d) sacrificed

10 *former* (line 41)
a) format
b) previous
c) future
d) formal

Spot the topic

Which of the following choices, a), b) or c), most adequately sums up the ideas of the *whole* paragraph?

1 *Para. 1* (lines 1–5)
a) The usefulness of cats to man.
b) The relationship between cats and man.
c) Man's indifference to and neglect of cats.

2 *Para. 2* (lines 6–11)
a) Bast
b) Bast and Bubastis
c) Bast: the most important Egyptian animal deity.

3 *Para. 3* (lines 12–17)
a) Early Egyptian beliefs and practices concerning cats.
b) Early Egyptian beliefs about living cats.
c) Early Egyptian beliefs about the powers of a living cat and how they always treated their animals kindly.

4 *Para. 4* (lines 18–23)
a) Egyptian mummies – their strange history.
b) An Egyptian cat cemetery was discovered.
c) Egyptian cat mummies and their fate.

5 *Para. 7* (lines 33–42)
a) Certain oriental beliefs and practices concerning cats.
b) Thai or Siamese cats.
c) Thai court ceremonies.

The history of chemistry

Primitive man found out by trial and error how to carry out a certain number of simple chemical changes, but under the ancient Egyptian civilization men learned how to work copper, tin, iron and precious metals; knew how to make pottery, glass, soap and colouring agents, and how to bleach and dye textile fabrics. These arts were the beginnings of the chemical industries of today. 5

The early scientific study of chemistry, known as alchemy, grew up in the first few centuries A.D. at Alexandria in Egypt. There two important things came together: one was the practical knowledge of the Egyptian workers in metals, pottery and dyes; the other was the learning of the earlier *Greek* philosophers, such as Hippocrates and Aristotle. At the same 10 time alchemy was much influenced by ideas from the East about magic and astrology – foretelling the future from the stars.

Greek philosophers regarded debate about the nature of matter as superior to experiment, and some held that all matter was made up of the same four 'elements' – earth, fire, air and water. Many people there- 15 fore thought that if these elements could be rearranged, one substance could be changed into another. For instance, a base metal could perhaps be turned into gold. The chief aim of the alchemists was to find a way of doing this.

Alchemy came under Arab influence when the armies of Islam conquered 20 Egypt during the seventh century. The Arabs carried its study into Western Europe when they advanced into Spain. Many Arabic words are still used in chemistry – 'alkali', 'alcohol' and even 'alchemy' itself, which means 'the art of Egypt'. The greatest Arab alchemist was Jabir ibn Hayyan, possibly the same person as Geber, author of two important books on 25 alchemy known from the Latin translations of the thirteenth century. Jabir claimed that mercury and sulphur were 'elements' like the four Greek ones. He said that all metals were composed of mercury and sulphur in different proportions. To change a base metal into gold required the proportions to be changed by the action of a mysterious substance which 30 came to be called 'the philosopher's stone'. Alchemists searched in vain for this substance for several hundred years.

Alchemy was studied widely in Europe during the twelfth and following centuries, and attracted the attention of many learned men. Though they were doomed to fail in their attempts to make gold, their work led to the 35 growth of a great deal of new chemical knowledge and of methods of making experiments. Many of the later European alchemists, however, were complete frauds who preyed upon trusting people by all sorts of tricks, and the subject fell into disrepute. By the first half of the sixteenth century, the aim of the alchemists had changed from the making of gold to the making of medicines. In particular they sought a fanciful substance called 'the elixir of life', a powerful medicine which was to cure all ills, and which some people thought would turn out to be the same substance as 'the philosopher's stone'. This phase of chemistry lasted till about 1700. 40

Ideas

Select the answer which is most accurate according to the information given in the passage.

1 Primitive man
a) knew nothing about chemistry.
b) succeeded in carrying out a few chemical processes.
c) failed to carry out any chemical processes.
d) knew how to work copper and make pottery.

2 The practical basis of several modern chemical industries was developed
a) by the ancient Egyptians.
b) by prehistoric man.
c) even before the ancient Egyptian civilization.
d) in the nineteenth century.

3 Alexandria was
a) the birthplace of the early science of chemistry.
b) the first chemical scientist.
c) the home of Greek philosophy.
d) named after the wife of Hippocrates.

4 The ancient Greeks
a) were superior to the Egyptians in chemical experiments.
b) were more fond of discussing theories than doing practical work.
c) were not interested in chemistry.
d) taught the Egyptians how to work metal, pottery and dyes.

5 Early alchemists tried to change
a) the element fire into water
b) all four elements into mercury.
c) the future using the stars.
d) inexpensive metals into gold.

6 The Arab conquerors
a) took alchemy to Egypt.
b) spread alchemy to Western Europe.
c) learnt 'the art of Egypt' in Spain.
d) overran the whole of Western Europe.

7   Jabir ibn Hayyan
a)   extended the Greek theories about the 'elements'.
b)   claimed that all metals were composed of four 'elements'.
c)   discovered 'the philosopher's stone'.
d)   wrote two important books on mathematics.

8   From the twelfth to the eighteenth centuries alchemy was
a)   successful in its objectives.
b)   a somewhat disreputable study.
c)   not studied.
d)   the most respected branch of philosophy.

9   Later alchemists
a)   changed gold into medicine.
b)   changed the philosopher's stone into medicine.
c)   directed their ambitions from gold to medicine.
d)   perfected the 'elixir of life'.

10 After 1700 chemistry
a)   was not studied.
b)   changed its aims and methods.
c)   did not last.
d)   became unfashionable.

Vocabulary

Find the following words in the passage and select the meaning you think
is *most likely* to correspond among the choices given.

1   *work* (line 3)
a)   exploit
b)   book
c)   exercise
d)   toil

2   *agents* (line 4)
a)   businessmen
b)   substances
c)   workers
d)   representatives

3   *bleach* (line 4)
a)   mould
b)   colour
c)   whiten
d)   hammer

4   *debate* (line 13)
a)   discussion
b)   doubt
c)   payment
d)   persuasion

5   *base* (line 29)
a)   bottom
b)   invaluable
c)   priceless
d)   common

6   *doomed* (line 35)
a)   died
b)   destined
c)   banned
d)   accustomed

7 *frauds* (line 38)
a) fools
b) deceivers
c) experts
d) forgers

9 *disrepute* (line 39)
a) disrespect
b) disrepair
c) discomfort
d) disuse

8 *preyed upon* (line 38)
a) ate as food
b) gave assistance to
c) begged from
d) made victims of

10 *phase* (line 44)
a) philosophy
b) science
c) period
d) aspect

Missing word summary

Fill in the numbered blanks from the selection of words given below. The correct choices will complete the sense of this summary of the reading passage.

Although the beginnings of metal and chemical industries are very ancient, it was [1] the first few centuries A.D. that chemistry became a more [2] study. This was at Alexandria in Egypt. Alchemy, [3] the early study was called, aimed principally at turning base metals [4] gold. By the sixteenth century, however, the study [5] more dedicated to the [6] of medicines. [7], they were trying to find 'the elixir of life' – a single medicine which [8] all types of sickness.

1 a) before
   b) until
   c) not until

5 a) had become
   b) began
   c) had been

2 a) systematic
   b) chemical
   c) practical

6 a) making
   b) make
   c) taking

3 a) for
   b) as
   c) because

7 a) Truly
   b) In particular
   c) Nevertheless

4 a) from
   b) like
   c) into

8 a) was curing
   b) would cure
   c) had cured

Passage 16

Electric fish

The idea of a fish being able to generate electricity strong enough to light lamp bulbs – or even to run a small electric motor – is almost unbelievable, but several kinds of fish are able to do this. Even more strangely, this curious power has been acquired in different ways by fish belonging to very different families. 5

Perhaps the best known are the electric rays, or torpedoes, of which several kinds live in warm seas. They possess on each side of the head, behind the eyes, a large organ consisting of a number of hexagonal shaped cells rather like a honeycomb. The cells are filled with a jelly-like substance, and contain a series of flat electric plates. One side, the negative side, of 10 each plate, is supplied with very fine nerves, connected with a main nerve coming from a special part of the brain. Current passes from the upper, positive side of the organ downwards to the negative, lower side. Generally it is necessary to touch the fish in two places, completing the circuit, in order to receive a shock. 15

The strength of this shock depends on the size of the fish, but newly born ones only about 5 centimetres across can be made to light the bulb of a pocket flashlight for a few moments, while a fully grown torpedo gives a shock capable of knocking a man down, and, if suitable wires are connected, will operate a small electric motor for several minutes. 20

Another famous example is the electric eel. This fish gives an even more powerful shock. The system is different from that of the torpedo in that the electric plates run longitudinally and are supplied with nerves from the spinal cord. Consequently, the current passes along the fish from head to tail. The electric organs of these fish are really altered muscles and like all 25 muscles are apt to tire, so they are not able to produce electricity for very long. People in some parts of South America who value the electric eel as food, take advantage of this fact by driving horses into the water against which the fish discharge their electricity. The horses are less affected than a man would be, and when the electric eels have exhausted themselves, 30 they can be caught without danger.

The electric catfish of the Nile and of other African fresh waters has a different system again by which current passes over the whole body from the tail to the head. The shock given by this arrangement is not so strong as the other two, but is none the less unpleasant. The electric catfish is a slow, 35 lazy fish, fond of gloomy places and grows to about 1 metre long; it is eaten by the Arabs in some areas.

The power of producing electricity may serve these fish both for defence

and attack. If a large enemy attacks, the shock will drive it away; but it
appears that the catfish and the electric eel use their current most often   40
against smaller fish, stunning them so that they can easily be overpowered.

Ideas

Say whether the following statements are true or false according to the
information given in the passage.

1 Some fish produce enough electricity to drive electric motors.
2 Electric rays are likely to be found in the Arctic Ocean.
3 The torpedo's electric cells are in its head.
4 Usually you will not get a shock by touching the electric ray in one
place only.
5 Only adult electric rays can produce electricity.
6 Electric rays are not strong enough to attack human beings.
7 The electric eel gives an even more powerful shock than the torpedo.
8 The electric plates on the electric eel are supplied with nerves from its
brain in the same way as those of the torpedo.
9 Men can withstand the shock of the electric eel less easily than horses
can.
10 The shock of the electric catfish is more unpleasant than that of the
torpedo or electric eel.

Vocabulary

Find the following words in the passage and select the meaning you think
is *most likely* to correspond among the choices given.

1 *run* (line 2)
a) go quickly
b) drive
c) supervise
d) race

2 *hexagonal* (line 8)
a) square
b) six-sided
c) oblong
d) eight-sided

3 *fine* (line 11)
a) thin
b) beautiful
c) very good
d) healthy

4 *current* (line 12)
a) flowing water
b) electricity
c) stream
d) heat

5 *value* (line 27)
a) like very much
b) price
c) worth
d) assess

6 *none the less* (line 35)
a) not so much as
b) more than
c) equally
d) nevertheless

7 *power* (line 38)
a) capability
b) strength
c) current
d) voltage

8 *serve* (line 38)
a) offer
b) be useful to
c) arrange
d) take care of

9 *drive* (line 39)
a) force
b) control
c) run
d) drill

10 *stunning* (line 41)
a) weakening
b) exciting
c) killing
d) destroying

Similar or different?

Say whether or not the statement is similar in meaning to the sentence from the passage indicated by the line number in brackets.

1 It is hardly strange that this power has been acquired by different families of fish in different ways. (lines 3–5)
2 They possess behind the head, instead of eyes, a large hexagonal organ, rather like a honeycomb. (lines 7–9)
3 Current travels in a downward direction from the upper side of the organ, which is positive, to the lower, or negative side. (lines 12–13)
4 A newly born one can be trained to provide light from a pocket flash-light while its fully grown partner knocks their victim down. (lines 16–19)
5 ... in that fish, the torpedo, the electric plates run lengthways. (lines 22–23)
6 Because the electric organs of these fish are altered muscles, they tire as muscles do, so they cannot produce electricity for very long periods of time. (lines 25–27)
7 The electric catfish shows an even further variation in its system of producing electricity, which involves the whole surface of the body. (lines 32–34)
8 Electric power may serve a dual purpose for these fish. (lines 38–39)

Dried food

Centuries ago, man discovered that removing moisture from food helps to
preserve it, and that the easiest way to do this is to expose the food to sun
and wind. In this way the North American Indians produce pemmican
(dried meat ground into powder and made into cakes), the Scandinavians
make stockfish and the Arabs dried dates and 'apricot leather'.   5

All foods contain water – cabbage and other leaf vegetables contain as
much as 93% water, potatoes and other root vegetables 80%, lean meat
75% and fish anything from 80% to 60% depending on how fatty it is.
If this water is removed, the activity of the bacteria which cause food to go
bad is checked.   10

Fruit is sun-dried in Asia Minor, Greece, Spain and other Mediterranean
countries, and also in California, South Africa and Australia. The methods
used vary, but in general, the fruit is spread out on trays in drying yards
in the hot sun. In order to prevent darkening, pears, peaches and apricots
are exposed to the fumes of burning sulphur before drying. Plums, for   15
making prunes, and certain varieties of grapes for making raisins and
currants, are dipped in an alkaline solution in order to crack the skins of
the fruit slightly and remove their wax coating, so increasing the rate of
drying.

Nowadays most foods are dried mechanically. The conventional method   20
of such dehydration is to put food in chambers through which hot air is
blown at temperatures of about 110 °C at entry to about 43 °C at exit.
This is the usual method for drying such things as vegetables, minced meat,
and fish.

Liquids such as milk, coffee, tea, soups and eggs may be dried by   25
pouring them over a heated horizontal steel cylinder or by spraying them
into a chamber through which a current of hot air passes. In the first
case, the dried material is scraped off the roller as a thin film which is
then broken up into small, though still relatively coarse flakes. In the
second process it falls to the bottom of the chamber as a fine powder.   30
Where recognizable pieces of meat and vegetables are required, as in soup,
the ingredients are dried separately and then mixed.

Dried foods take up less room and weigh less than the same food packed
in cans or frozen, and they do not need to be stored in special conditions.
For these reasons they are invaluable to climbers, explorers and soldiers   35
in battle, who have little storage space. They are also popular with housewives because it takes so little time to cook them. Usually it is just a case
of replacing the dried-out moisture with boiling water.

Passage 17

Ideas

Select the answer which is most accurate according to the information given in the passage.

1   The open-air method of drying food
a)   is the one most commonly used today.
b)   was invented by the American Indians.
c)   has been known for hundreds of years.
d)   tends to be unhygienic.

2   The water content
a)   does not vary from food to food.
b)   is greater in green vegetables than in lean meat.
c)   is greater in fish than in vegetables.
d)   has never been accurately calculated.

3   Bacteria which cause food to go bad
a)   cannot live in sunlight.
b)   are killed by drying.
c)   are in no way dependent on the water content.
d)   have their activity greatly reduced by drying.

4   Fruit is sun dried
a)   always by the same method.
b)   generally on trays.
c)   in every country in the world.
d)   by spreading it out under glass panels.

5   Sulphur fumes are used before drying some fruits
a)   to dry them more quickly.
b)   to preserve their colour.
c)   to prevent the skin from cracking.
d)   to kill off bacteria.

6   Nowadays vegetables are most commonly dried
a)   on horizontal cylinders.
b)   in hot-air chambers.
c)   in the sun and wind.
d)   using the open tray method.

7   Powdered coffee is made
a)   by spraying the liquid over a cylinder.
b)   in one of two different ways.
c)   in the same way as minced meat.
d)   by passing through a grinding machine.

8 If soup requires recognizable pieces of meat, they are
a) treated separately.
b) allowed to fall to the bottom of the drying chamber.
c) mixed in later as a fine powder.
d) sold separately in sealed plastic bags.

9 Dried foods
a) are often packed in cans or frozen.
b) are used by soldiers and climbers.
c) need more storage space than soldiers usually have available.
d) are much cheaper than canned or frozen products.

10 Housewives like dried foods because they
a) are quick to prepare.
b) taste better.
c) can be preserved by boiling in water.
d) look fresh and appetizing when cooked.

Vocabulary

Find the following words in the passage and select the meaning you think is *most likely* to correspond among the choices given.

1 *expose to* (line 2)
a) leave out in
b) protect from
c) open out
d) demonstrate to

2 *stockfish* (line 5)
a) dried fish
b) salted fish
c) cooked fish
d) stored fish

3 *apricot leather* (line 5)
a) dried dates
b) dried apricots
c) dried leather
d) cloth made from dried fruit skins

4 *checked* (line 10)
a) looked over
b) supervised
c) stopped
d) verified

5 *prunes* (line 16)
a) dried plums
b) dried sulphur
c) types of grape
d) fruit cuttings

6 *conventional* (line 20)
a) most common
b) old-fashioned
c) hygienic
d) obsolete

7 *dehydration* (line 21)
a) heating
b) airing
c) mechanization
d) drying

8 *relatively* (line 29)
a) in the same way
b) fairly
c) similarly
d) extremely

Passage 17

9   *invaluable* (line 35)
a) worthless
b) inexpensive
c) very useful
d) free of charge

10 *case* (line 37)
a) box
b) matter
c) cooking container
d) example

Spot the topic

Choose the phrase or sentence a), b) or c) which most adequately identifies the main point made by the paragraph or paragraphs indicated.

1   *Para. 1* (lines 1–5)
a) Drying fruit.
b) Different methods of preserving things.
c) Preserving food by drying.

2   *Para. 2* (lines 6–10)
a) The relationship between water content and food decay.
b) The relative water content of different types of food.
c) The water content of vegetables.

3   *Para. 3* (lines 11–19)
a) The use of sulphur in preserving food.
b) The sun-drying method of preserving fruit.
c) The relative geographical distribution of food preservation techniques.

4   *Paras. 4 and 5* (lines 20–32)
a) Heat drying of liquids and minced meat.
b) Hot-air chamber drying of food.
c) The three principal methods of mechanical food drying.

5   *Para. 6* (lines 33–38)
a) The general convenience of dried foods.
b) Why housewives like dried foods.
c) The advantages of canned, frozen and dried foods.

65

Passage 18

The United Nations

In one very long sentence, the introduction to the U.N. Charter expresses
the ideals and the common aims of all the peoples whose governments
joined together to form the U.N.

'We the peoples of the U.N. determined to save succeeding generations
from the scourge of war, which twice in our lifetime has brought untold   5
suffering to mankind, and to reaffirm faith in fundamental rights, in the
dignity and worth of the human person, in the equal rights of men and
women and of nations large and small, and to establish conditions under
which justice and respect for the obligations arising from treaties and other
sources of international law can be maintained, and to promote social   10
progress and better standards of life in larger freedom, and for these ends,
to practise tolerance and live together in peace with one another as good
neighbours, and to unite our strength to maintain international peace
and security, and to ensure, by the acceptance of principles and the
institution of methods, that armed force shall not be used, save in the   15
common interest, and to employ international machinery for the
promotion of economic and social advancement of all peoples, have
resolved to combine our efforts to accomplish these aims.'

The name 'United Nations' is accredited to U.S. President Franklin
D. Roosevelt, and the first group of representatives of member states met   20
and signed a declaration of common intent on New Year's Day in 1942.
Representatives of five powers worked together to draw up proposals,
completed at Dumbarton Oaks in 1944. These proposals, modified after
deliberation at the conference on International Organization in San
Francisco which began in April 1945, were finally agreed on and signed   25
as the U.N. Charter by 50 countries on 26 June 1945. Poland, not represented at the conference, signed the Charter later and was added to the
list of original members. It was not until that autumn, however, after
the Charter had been ratified by China, France, the U.S.S.R., the U.K.
and the U.S. and by a majority of the other participants that the U.N.   30
offficially came into existence. The date was 24 October, now universally
celebrated as United Nations Day.

The essential functions of the U.N. are to maintain international peace
and security, to develop friendly relations among nations, to cooperate
internationally in solving international economic, social, cultural and human 35
problems, promoting respect for human rights and fundamental freedoms
and to be a centre for co-ordinating the actions of nations in attaining
these common ends.

Passage 18

No country takes precedence over another in the U.N. Each member's
rights and obligations are the same. All must contribute to the peaceful   40
settlement of international disputes, and members have pledged to refrain
from the threat or use of force against other states. Though the U.N. has
no right to intervene in any state's internal affairs, it tries to ensure that
non-member states act according to its principles of international peace
and security. UN members must offer every assistance in an approved   45
U.N. action and in no way assist states against which the U.N. is taking
preventive or enforcement action.

Ideas

Select the answer which is most accurate according to the information
given in the passage.

1   The first stated aim of the U.N. was
a)   to supervise peace treaties.
b)   to revise international laws.
c)   to prevent a third world war.
d)   to assist the 'third world' countries.

2   Under its Charter, the U.N. guarantees
a)   never to use arms.
b)   to employ international machines.
c)   better standards of life.
d)   to promote economic and social advancement.

3   President Roosevelt
a)   probably devised the name 'The United Nations'.
b)   was given the name 'The United Nations'.
c)   established 'The United Nations'.
d)   was a credit to 'The United Nations'.

4   Dumbarton Oaks was the place where
a)   the U.N. first met.
b)   representatives of five powers formulated basic suggestions.
c)   the final proposals were agreed on and the Charter signed.
d)   50 countries signed the U.N. Charter.

5   The U.N. came into existence fully in
a)   1942.
b)   1944.
c)   1945.
d)   1940.

6   United Nations Day is celebrated on
a)   24 October.
b)   24 April.
c)   26 October.
d)   26 June.

7   The essential functions of the U.N.
a)   are limited to discussions and debates.
b)   include co-ordinating actions where necessary.
c)   are only concerned with human rights.
d)   are economic and cultural.

8   Large member countries like China and the U.S.
a)   have precedence over small countries like Poland.
b)   have more freedom in the U.N. than Poland.
c)   provide 75% of U.N. running costs.
d)   have the same rights and duties as other members.

9   A country's domestic policies
a)   cannot be forcibly changed by the U.N.
b)   are often investigated by the U.N.
c)   are often enforced by the U.N.
d)   are not allowed to benefit from U.N. advice or assistance.

10 A member country cannot ally itself with
a)   other U.N. member countries.
b)   other countries not members of the U.N.
c)   countries defying the U.N.
d)   states against which the U.N. has ever taken preventive or enforcement
     action.

Vocabulary

Find the following words in the passage and select the meaning you think
is *most likely* to correspond among the choices given.

1   *succeeding* (line 4)
a)   following
b)   successful
c)   past
d)   struggling

4   *common* (line 21)
a)   usual
b)   low
c)   ordinary
d)   shared

2   *obligations* (line 9)
a)   duties
b)   thanks
c)   results
d)   politeness

5   *intent* (line 21)
a)   concentration
b)   hope
c)   purpose
d)   anxiety

3   *save* (line 15)
a)   rescue
b)   except
c)   preserve
d)   even

6   *powers* (line 22)
a)   countries
b)   strengths
c)   armies
d)   delegates

7 *deliberation* (line 24)	9 *ends* (line 38)
a) debate	a) means
b) freedom	b) stops
c) purposefulness	c) conclusions
d) private agreements	d) objectives
8 *ratified* (line 29)	10 *pledged* (line 41)
a) challenged	a) agreed
b) made official	b) obliged
c) distributed	c) supposed
d) attacked	d) refused

Similar or different?

Say whether or not the statement is similar in meaning to the sentence from the passage indicated by the line number in brackets.

N.B. Because the sentence from the introduction is so long, numbers 1, 2 and 3 are only *extracts* from it.

1   ... to create a situation which supports justice and the fulfilment of international agreements (lines 8–10, ... to establish ... maintained)
2   ... by accepting principles and instituting methods, to prevent the use of arms at all times to save the common interest (lines 14–16, ... to ensure ... interest)
3   ... to create organs which function on a cooperative basis to encourage the economic and social progress of every nation (lines 16–17, ... to employ ... peoples)
4   In spite of not assisting at the Charter signing ceremony, Poland is nevertheless on the list of original members (lines 26–28)
5   Having no right to interfere in any state's home affairs limits the U.N.'s power in international peace and security (lines 42–45)

Pottery

Pottery is the name given to all kinds of pots and utensils made from clay and other minerals when they have been 'fired', that is, hardened by heat in the potter's kiln. Articles made of pottery include plates, cups and saucers, cooking dishes, wall and floor tiles, chemical storage jars, bathroom fittings, filters, drain pipes, electrical insulators and ornaments for the home. 5

Pottery is one of the oldest crafts, which began to be practised as soon as man learned to control fire, and long before the melting of metals. It enabled him from very early times to make vessels for storing and cooking food, for carrying water, and for ritual burial purposes. Early vessels were 10 shaped by hand and probably 'fired' in a big bonfire by covering them over with dried grass and dead branches, which were then set alight.

A great advance in pottery followed the invention of the potter's wheel and the kiln. It is not certainly known where the potter's wheel was first used, but it is thought that by about 3500 B.C. potters in Central Asia 15 were using some kind of wheel. From there its use spread west and east to Egypt, Crete, China – and then to Ancient Greece and Rome.

At first the wheel was nothing more than a small disc, turned on a pivot by hand, but later it was improved by raising it and providing it with a larger circular platform near the ground as well which could be 20 rotated by the potter with his feet. Such a wheel was probably in use in Egypt by about 200 B.C., though this is only conjecture; but it was certainly still in use in Europe at the beginning of the nineteenth century. In the eighteenth century, however, the potter's wheel was improved so that it could be worked by a treadle, or turned by an assistant. Modern 25 potters' wheels are power driven.

There are three principal ways articles may be made of pottery. They may be simply shaped by hand. They may be thrown on the potter's wheel and shaped against the spin with the fingers or some scraping tool. Thirdly, the wet clay may be put in a pre-shaped 'form' of plaster-of- 30 Paris.

After the pots have been made, they are slowly baked in the kiln. This produces chemical changes in the clay which have a hardening effect. The time taken for firing pottery varies with the size of the kiln and the type of clay. It can take anything from 24 hours to as long as 2 weeks. 35

If pottery is to hold water, it must be 'glazed', since clay is porous by nature. Glaze consists of the raw materials of glass, ground together and mixed with water to a creamy consistency. The glaze is sprayed on to the

pot which is then heated in the kiln again until it is, in effect, covered with
a very thin layer of glass. This seals the pores in the clay and gives us the   40
versatile table and oven dishes we know so well today.

Ideas

Select the answer which is most accurate according to the information given
in the passage.

1   Pottery is the name given to
a)   all kinds of utensils.
b)   all kinds of pots and utensils.
c)   domestic fittings and table dishes.
d)   things made of baked clay or other minerals.

2   The early making of pottery
a)   pre-dated the discovery of fire.
b)   post-dated the smelting of metals.
c)   was dependent on the control of fire.
d)   avoided the need for storing and treating food.

3   Before the invention of the potter's wheel
a)   pottery vessels were shaped by hand.
b)   it was impossible to make pottery vessels.
c)   pottery vessels were shaped by heating in a bonfire.
d)   pottery could only be obtained from Central Asia.

4   The first potter's wheel was invented
a)   in Central Asia.
b)   in Egypt.
c)   in Ancient Greece.
d)   probably before 3500 B.C.

5   The ancient Greeks and Romans
a)   did not use the potter's wheel.
b)   learned about the potter's wheel from elsewhere.
c)   did not make pottery.
d)   carried the potter's wheel to Egypt, Crete and China.

6   Improvements to the potter's wheel
a)   came only in the twentieth century.
b)   have never really been successful.
c)   have been concerned with motive power methods mainly.
d)   ceased after 200 B.C.

7   A foot-operated potter's wheel was in use in Egypt
a)   certainly by 2000 B.C.
b)   probably by the beginning of the nineteenth century.
c)   for a short period in the second century A.D.
d)   perhaps around 200 B.C.

8   The three ways articles can be made of pottery are
a)   spinning, moulding and ' throwing '.
b)   ' throwing ', hand shaping and on a wheel.
c)   hand shaping, ' throwing ' on a wheel, and moulding in a 'form'.
d)   are becoming increasingly sophisticated.

9   The time taken for firing pottery varies according to
a)   the type of clay the kiln is made of.
b)   the type of clay and the size of kiln it is baked in.
c)   the type of kiln the pottery is baked in.
d)   atmospheric conditions.

10 The glaze on a pottery vessel
a)   keeps the clay soft.
b)   prevents the clay from becoming porous.
c)   prevents the clay from allowing moisture to pass through its pores.
d)   makes it more attractive to look at.

Vocabulary

Find the following words in the passage and select the meaning you think
is *most likely* to correspond among the choices given.

1   *bonfire* (line 11)
a)   oven
b)   kiln
c)   outdoor fire
d)   kitchen fire

2   *pivot* (line 19)
a)   axle
b)   wheel
c)   lever
d)   base

3   *platform* (line 20)
a)   stage
b)   foot board
c)   raised seat
d)   support

4   *conjecture* (line 22)
a)   primitive
b)   false rumour
c)   guessing
d)   fiction

5   *treadle* (line 25)
a)   handle
b)   pedal
c)   motor
d)   step

6   *spin* (line 29)
a)   turn quickly
b)   direction of turning
c)   revolve
d)   hand tool

7   *'form'* (line 30)
a)   mould
b)   bench
c)   appearance
d)   figure

8   *firing* (line 34)
a)   shooting
b)   baking
c)   burning
d)   covering

9 *pores* (line 40)
a) colours
b) designs
c) small holes
d) lines

10 *versatile* (line 41)
a) fragile
b) multi-purpose
c) porous
d) reversible

Similar or different?

Say whether or not the statement is similar in meaning to the sentence from the passage indicated by the line number in brackets.

1   Anything made from clay is called 'pottery'. (lines 1–3)
2   Early vessels were probably covered with dry grass and brushwood which was then set alight to 'fire' them. (lines 10–12)
3   The invention of the potter's wheel and the kiln made no small contribution to the art of pottery. (lines 13–14)
4   It is not by any means certain that such a wheel was in use in Egypt by about 200 B.C., though it most probably was. (lines 21–22)
5   The size of the clay article, and the type of kiln are just two of the factors which affect the time taken for firing pottery. (lines 33–35)
6   If pottery is filled with water, it will become 'glazed', as clay is naturally porous. (lines 36–37)

Pasteurization

The value of heat for the preservation of food has been known for thousands of years, but it was not realized until the nineteenth century that a very mild heat treatment far below the boiling point, made liquid foods such as milk keep much longer. The discovery followed the work of the French scientist Louis Pasteur on wine and beer.   5

The process, called after him 'pasteurization', is a carefully controlled mild heat treatment. It was found that the process served two purposes; it prevented the souring of milk, and it destroyed the dangerous disease germs which sometimes occur in this product. These germs include the bacteria which cause tuberculosis, undulant fever, typhoid and paratyphoid   10
fevers, dysentery, diphtheria, scarlet fever and septic sore throat.

It has long been known to bacteria experts that the tubercle bacillus* is the germ in milk which most strongly resists heat treatment. To destroy this organism it is necessary to heat milk to about 60 °C. for 15 minutes, and its destruction has always been taken as a way of testing the efficiency   15
of pasteurization. A heat treatment of this kind destroys about 99% of the common bacteria in milk, including nearly all those which cause milk to turn sour.

To ensure the certain destruction of tuberculosis and other disease germs in milk, it must be held at a fixed temperature for a fixed time. In Britain,   20
for example, these conditions were defined by law in 1923 as 63–66 °C. for 30 minutes. This became known as the 'holder' process, since the raw milk had to be pumped into a large tank, heated to just over 63 °C., held in the tank for half an hour and then pumped out and cooled. This was a slow process and required a very cumbersome plant, so scientists worked   25
for many years to produce a simpler, more convenient method, with less bulky equipment.

The latest method, officially approved in Britain in 1949, is known as the high-temperature-short-time, or H.T.S.T. method. It has now almost entirely replaced the 'holder' process. In the H.T.S.T. system, the milk   30
flows continuously through many sections of thin stainless steel pipes. During the process, the milk is held at 72 °C. for at least 15 seconds, then, as it cools, the heat it loses is used, in part, to raise the temperature of the incoming milk in a device called a 'heat-exchanger'.

Efficient pasteurization may reduce the bacteria in raw milk from, say   35
one million to only a few thousand per cubic centimetre. The bacteria left are chemically mostly of the inert type, that is, they either do not

* _tubercle bacillus:_ the name for the bacteria which cause tuberculosis – an often fatal lung disease.

sour milk at all, or sour it only slowly. Very strict cleanliness is, however, essential and all pipes, containers and bottling machines in a pasteurizing plant must be cleaned and sterilized daily. If the slightest trace of dirt remains all the benefits of pasteurization are wasted.

40

Ideas

Say whether the following statements are true or false according to the information given in the passage.

1 It was not until the nineteenth century that people realized that heat could help preserve food.
2 Without heat treatment, milk may be seriously harmful to health.
3 Pasteurization destroys nearly all common bacteria in milk.
4 The 'holder' process was so called because the milk was 'held' in a tank for half an hour.
5 Scientists found it quite easy to invent a simpler more convenient process than the 'holder' method.
6 H.T.S.T. stands for Health-Tested for a Short Time.
7 The H.T.S.T. system has now been almost replaced by the 'holder' process.
8 In the H.T.S.T. system, the milk is kept in a holder tank at 72 °C. for at least 15 seconds.
9 Raw milk may contain one million bacteria per cubic centimetre.
10 If the pasteurization plant is strictly cleaned every week, the benefit of the process will not be wasted.

Vocabulary

Find the following words in the passage and select the meaning you think is *most likely* to correspond among the choices given.

1 *realized* (line 2)
a) proved
b) put into practice
c) understood
d) sold for cash

2 *mild* (line 3)
a) slow
b) strong
c) low
d) kind

3 *keep* (line 4)
a) save
b) stay fresh
c) remain hot
d) preserve

4 *served* (line 7)
a) obeyed
b) fulfilled
c) needed
d) offered

5 *taken* (line 15)
a) carried away
b) accepted
c) stolen
d) noted down

6 *certain* (line 19)
a) limited amount of
b) assured
c) partial
d) convinced

7 *cumbersome* (line 25)
a) inconveniently large
b) difficult to carry
c) ugly
d) expensive

9 *strict* (line 38)
a) conscientious
b) punishing
c) severe
d) harsh

8 *inert* (line 37)
a) inactive
b) interior
c) quite active
d) indestructible

10 *trace* (line 40)
a) small amount
b) blockage
c) line
d) seek out

Spot the topic

Choose the phrase or sentence a), b) or c) which most adequately identifies the main point made by the paragraph or paragraphs indicated.

1 *Para. 2* (lines 6–11)
a) The two effects of pasteurization on milk.
b) Pasteurization and the souring of milk.
c) Mild heat treatment of milk prevents ill-health.

2 *Para. 3* (lines 12–18)
a) The tubercle bacillus as a criterion for sterilization.
b) Pasteurization and lactic streptococci.
c) Time and temperature criteria for the souring of milk.

3 *Para. 4* (lines 19–27)
a) The 'holder' process.
b) The 1923 law against tuberculosis in Britain.
c) The superiority of the 'holder' process.

4 *Para. 5* (lines 28–34)
a) The 'heat exchanger'.
b) The H.T.S.T. method.
c) The disadvantage of the high-temperature process.

5 *Para. 6* (lines 35–41)
a) The importance of cleanliness for effective pasteurization.
b) Pasteurization kills all germs.
c) Pipes, containers and bottling machines, their manufacture and maintenance.

Modern surgery

The need for a surgical operation, especially an emergency operation, almost always comes as a severe shock to the patient and his family. Despite modern advances, most people still have an irrational fear of hospitals and anaesthetics. Patients do not often believe they really *need* surgery – cutting into a part of the body as opposed to treatment with drugs.   5

In the early years of this century there was little specialization in surgery. A good surgeon was capable of performing almost every operation that had been devised up to that time. Today the situation is different. Operations are now being carried out that were not even dreamed of fifty years ago. The heart can be safely opened and its valves repaired. Clogged blood   10
vessels can be cleaned out, and broken ones mended or replaced. A lung, the whole stomach, or even part of the brain can be removed and still permit the patient to live a comfortable and satisfactory life. However, not every surgeon wants to, or is qualified to carry out *every* type of modern operation.   15

The scope of surgery has increased remarkably in this century. Its safety has increased too. Deaths from most operations are about 20% of what they were in 1910 and surgery has been extended in many directions, for example to certain types of birth defects in newborn babies, and, at the other end of the scale, to life-saving operations for the octogenarian. The   20
hospital stay after surgery has been shortened to as little as a week for most major operations. Most patients are out of bed on the day after an operation and may be back at work in two or three weeks.

Many developments in modern surgery are almost incredible. They include the replacement of damaged blood vessels with simulated ones   25
made of plastic; the replacement of heart valves with plastic substitutes; the transplanting of tissues such as the lens of the eye; the invention of the artificial kidney to clean the blood of poisons at regular intervals and the development of heart and lung machines to keep patients alive during very long operations. All these things open a hopeful vista for the future of   30
surgery.

One of the most revolutionary areas of modern surgery is that of organ transplants. Until a few years ago, no person, except an identical twin, was able to accept into his body the tissues of another person without reacting against them and eventually killing them. Recently, however, it   35
has been discovered that with the use of x-rays and special drugs, it is possible to graft tissues from one person to another which will survive for periods of a year or more. Kidneys have been successfully transplanted

between non-identical twins. Heart and lung transplants have been reason-
ably successful in animals, though rejection problems in humans have yet   40
to be solved.

'Spare parts' surgery, the simple routine replacement of all worn-out
organs by new ones, is still a dream of the distant future. As yet, surgery
is not ready for such miracles. In the meantime, you can be happy if your
doctor says to you, 'Yes, I think it is possible to operate on you for this   45
condition.'

Ideas

Select the answer which is most accurate according to the information given
in the passage.

1   Most people are afraid of being operated on
a)   in spite of improvements in modern surgery.
b)   because they think modern drugs are dangerous.
c)   because they do not believe they need anaesthetics.
d)   unless it is an emergency operation.

2   Surgeons in the early years of this century, compared with modern
     ones,
a)   had less to learn about surgery.
b)   needed more knowledge.
c)   could perform every operation known today.
d)   were more trusted by their patients.

3   Open heart surgery has been possible
a)   only in the last fifty years.
b)   from prehistoric times.
c)   since the nineteenth century.
d)   since the invention of valves.

4   A patient can still live a comfortable and satisfactory life, even after
     the removal of
a)   his brain.
b)   his lungs.
c)   a major organ such as the stomach or one lung.
d)   part of the stomach or the whole liver.

5   Modern surgeons
a)   do not like to perform operations of the new type.
b)   are not as highly qualified as the older ones.
c)   are obliged to specialize more than their predecessors.
d)   often perform operations which are not really needed.

6   Today, compared with 1910
a)   five times fewer patients die after being operated on.
b)   20% fewer of all operation patients die.

c) 20% of all operation patients recover.
d) operation deaths have increased by 20%.

7   Some of the more astonishing innovations in modern surgery include
a)   ear, nose and throat transplants.
b)   valveless plastic hearts.
c)   plastic heart valves.
d)   leg transplants.

8   The main difficulty with organ transplants is
a)   it is difficult to find organs of exactly the same size.
b)   only identical twins can give permission for their organs to be exchanged.
c)   the body's tendency to reject alien tissues.
d)   the patient is not allowed to use drugs after them.

9   'Spare parts' surgery
a)   has yet to be come a reality.
b)   will be available in the near furure.
c)   is only possible for animals.
d)   has been replaced by modern drug treatments.

10 You can be happy if your surgeon can operate because it means
a)   he thinks your condition may be curable.
b)   he is a good doctor.
c)   he knows you will survive.
d)   you are getting better already.

Vocabulary

Find the following words in the passage and select the meaning you think
is *most likely* to correspond among the choices given.

1   *severe* (line 2)
a)   strong
b)   bad-tempered
c)   disciplined
d)   cut

2   *advances* (line 3)
a)   financial grants
b)   attacks
c)   improvements
d)   loans

3   *irrational* (line 3)
a)   logical
b)   understandable
c)   unreasonable
d)   unusual

4   *clogged* (line 10)
a)   blocked
b)   unwashed
c)   covered
d)   clean

Passage 21

5 *permit* (line 13)
a) authorize
b) allow
c) give permission to
d) pass

6 *octogenarian* (line 20)
a) eighteen-year-old
b) person in his eighties
c) patient having eighth operation
d) eye specialist

7 *simulated* (line 25)
a) artificial
b) dissimilar
c) simplified
d) lengthened

8 *vista* (line 30)
a) support
b) prospect
c) history
d) visit

9 *revolutionary* (line 32)
a) arguable
b) politically active
c) interestingly new
d) violent

10 *routine* (line 42)
a) difficult
b) boring
c) everyday
d) scheduled

Similar or different?

Say whether or not the statement is similar in meaning to the sentence from the passage indicated by the line number in brackets.

1 Operations are now being carried out that no one even considered fifty years ago. (lines 8–9)
2 Repair and replacement of a lung, the whole stomach, or even part of the brain, allow patients to lead comfortable and satisfactory lives. (lines 11–13)
3 A large number of modern advances in surgery are difficult to believe. (line 24)
4 Until fairly recently, no one except an identical twin could accept another person's tissues into his body without being killed by these tissues. (lines 33–35)
5 The replacement of the heart and the lungs in animals has been completely successful, though the problem with humans is that they reject the idea of organ transplants. (lines 38–40)

80

Passage 22

Smoking and cancer

Americans smoke six thousand *million* cigarettes every year (1970 figures).
This is roughly the equivalent of 4,195 cigarettes a year for every person in
the country of 18 years of age or more. It is estimated that 51% of American
men smoke compared with 34% of American women.

Since 1939, numerous scientific studies have been conducted to determine 5
whether smoking is a health hazard. The trend of the evidence has been
consistent and indicates that there is a serious health risk. Research teams
have conducted studies that show beyond all reasonable doubt that tobacco
smoking, particularly cigarette smoking is associated with a shortened life
expectancy. 10

Cigarette smoking is believed by most research workers in this field to be
an important factor in the development of cancer of the lungs and cancer
of the throat and is believed to be related to cancer of the bladder and the
oral cavity. Male cigarette smokers have a higher death rate from heart
disease than non-smoking males. (Female smokers are thought to be less 15
affected because they do not breathe in the smoke so deeply.) The
majority of physicians and researchers consider these relationships proved
to their satisfaction and say, 'Give up smoking, If you don't smoke – don't
start!'

Some competent physicians and research workers – though their small 20
number is dwindling even further – are less sure of the effect of cigarette
smoking on health. They consider the increase in respiratory diseases and
various forms of cancer may possibly be explained by other factors in the
complex human environment – atmospheric pollution, increased nervous
stress, chemical substances in processed food, or chemical pesticides that 25
are now being used by farmers in vast quantities to destroy insects and small
animals. Smokers who develop cancer or lung diseases, they say, may also,
by coincidence, live in industrial areas, or eat more canned food. Gradually,
however, research is isolating all other possible factors and proving them
to be statistically irrelevant. 30

Apart from statistics, it might be helpful to look at what smoking tobacco
actually does to the human body. Smoke is a mixture of gases, vaporized
chemicals, minute particles of ash, and other solids. There is also nicotine,
which is a powerful poison, and black tar. As the smoke is breathed in, all
these components form deposits on the membranes of the lungs. One point 35
of concentration is where the air tube, or bronchus, divides. Most lung
cancer begins at this point.

Smoking also affects the heart and blood vessels. It is known to be

81

related to Beurger's disease, a narrowing of the small veins in the hands and
feet that can cause great pain and lead even to amputation of limbs.   40
Smokers also die much more often from heart disease.

   While all tobacco smoking affects life expectancy and health, cigarette
smoking appears to have a much greater effect than cigar or pipe smoking.
However, *nicotine* consumption is not diminished by the latter forms, and
current research indicates a causal relationship between *all* forms of smok-   45
ing and cancer of the mouth and throat. Filters and low tar tobacco
are claimed to make smoking to some extent safer, but they can only
marginally reduce, not eliminate the hazards.

Ideas

Say whether the following statements are true or false according to the
information given in the passage.

1   According to 1970 figures there are twice as many men smokers as
    women smokers in the United States.
2   In 1939 numerous scientific studies proved smoking causes fatal
    diseases.
3   In spite of consistent evidence that smoking is most probably a serious
    health risk, scientists are still not in a position to prove absolutely
    that it actually causes life-shortening diseases.
4   Some research workers in the field of smoking and disease do not
    believe smoking to be necessarily an important factor in the develop-
    ment of cancer of the lungs and larynx.
5   Female smokers are probably less affected by heart disease because
    they inhale the smoke less deeply.
6   A small number of physicians and research workers think that the
    increase in respiratory diseases and various forms of cancer may be
    caused by other factors in the complex human environment.
7   One of the major difficulties of research into human health problems is
    the difficulty of isolating particular, individual factors from the com-
    plex human environment.
8   Tobacco smoke is a mixture of two poisonous gases.
9   Since the elements of tobacco smoke are deposited in large amounts at
    the point where the bronchus divides, and since this is the point where
    most lung cancer starts, we can logically conclude that tobacco smoking
    is definitely the cause of lung cancer.
10 Cigar and pipe smokers consume marginally less nicotine than cigarette
    smokers.

Passage 22

Vocabulary

Find the following words in the passage and select the meaning you think
is *most likely* to correspond among the choices given.

1   *roughly* (line 2)
a) approximately
b) rudely
c) impolitely
d) exactly

2   *consistent* (line 7)
a) slow
b) conclusively proved
c) steadily similar
d) mixed

3   *dwindling* (line 21)
a) insignificant
b) increasing
c) decreasing
d) investigating

4   *processed* (line 25)
a) factory treated
b) hygienically packed
c) stored
d) constructed

5   *pesticides* (line 25)
a) fertilizers
b) animal foods
c) pest killers
d) weed killers

6   *develop* (line 27)
a) are attacked by
b) encourage
c) progress
d) improve

7   *deposits* (line 35)
a) accumulations
b) protective coatings
c) savings
d) gases

8   *concentration* (line 36)
a) irritation
b) maximum build-up
c) attention
d) division

9   *amputation* (line 40)
a) cutting off
b) disease
c) curing
d) discomfort

10 *marginally* (line 48)
a) greatly
b) slightly
c) unevenly
d) written in the margin

Missing word summary

Fill in the numbered blanks from the selection of words given below. The
correct choices will complete the sense of this summary of the reading
passage.

Nearly half the [1] population of the U.S.A. are smokers, in [2] the fact
that medical research has shown beyond reasonable doubt that smoking is
associated with poor health. One very important disease with [3] smoking
is thought to be connected, is [4]. [5], a few doctors think such things as
bronchitis and cancer have other [6], [7] their view is not well-supported
statistically. Although all forms of [8] are almost certainly dangerous,
cigarettes appear to be the most harmful.

1 a) male
   b) total
   c) adult

2 a) addition to
   b) spite of
   c) agreement with

3 a) whom
   b) what
   c) which

4 a) bladder
   b) cancer
   c) oral cavity

5 a) However
   b) Also
   c) Indeed

6 a) results
   b) effects
   c) causes

7 a) and
   b) but
   c) so

8 a) disease
   b) smoking
   c) cancer

Rabies

Rabies is an ordinarily infectious disease of the central nervous system, caused by a virus* and, as a rule, spread chiefly by domestic dogs and wild flesh-eating animals. Man and all warm-blooded animals are susceptible to rabies. The people of ancient Egypt, Greece and Rome ascribed rabies to evil spirits because ordinarily gentle and friendly animals suddenly became   5
vicious and violent without evident cause and, after a period of maniacal behaviour, became paralysed and died.

Experiments carried out in Europe in the early nineteenth century of injecting saliva* from a rabid dog into a normal dog proved that the disease was infectious. Preventive steps, such as the destruction of stray dogs, were   10
taken and by 1826 the disease was permanently eliminated in Norway, Sweden and Denmark. Though urban centres on the continent of Europe were cleared several times during the nineteenth century, they soon became reinfected since rabies was uncontrolled among wild animals.

During the early stages of the disease, a rabid animal is most dangerous   15
because it appears normal and friendly, but it will bite at the slightest provocation. The virus is present in the salivary glands and passes into the saliva so that the bite of the infected animal introduces the virus into a fresh wound. If no action is taken, the virus may become established in the central nervous system and finally attack the brain. The incubation   20
period varies from ten days to eight months or more, and the disease develops more quickly the nearer to the brain the wound is. Most infected dogs become restless, nervous, and irritable and vicious, then depressed and paralysed. With this type of rabies, the dog's death is inevitable and usually occurs within three to five days after the onset of the symptoms.   25

In 1881 Pasteur discovered that the infective agent of rabies could be recovered from the brain of an animal that had died of rabies. He experimented on rabbits and developed a new variety of rabies which could safely be used for vaccination. A series of injections of this new virus made dogs resistant to the common natural virus. For the first time in 1885 the   30
substance was used in a desperate attempt to save a badly bitten boy. The theory was that if dogs could be protected in a two-week period, the longer incubation period of human beings would allow the development of a high degree of protection before the potential onset of the disease. The treatment proved successful and the boy remained well.   35

* *virus:* disease-carrying organism much smaller than bacteria.
  saliva: moisture which foams in the mouths of humans and other animals.
  vaccination: protection from a disease by the injection of dead of weakened germs which cause that disease.

Anti-rabies vaccine is widely used nowadays in two ways. Dogs may be given three-year protection against the disease by one powerful injection, while persons who have been bitten by rabid animals are given a course of daily injections over a week or ten days. The mortality rate from all types of bites from rabid animals has dropped from 9% to 0.5%. In rare cases, the vaccine will not prevent rabies in human beings because the virus produces the disease before the person's body has time to build up enough resistance. Because of this, immediate vaccination is essential for anyone bitten by an animal observed acting strangely and the animal should be captured circumspectly, and examined professionally or destroyed.

40

45

Ideas

Say whether the following statements are true or false according to the information given in the passage.

1   Any animal can be infected with rabies.
2   The disease was not proved to be infectious until the nineteenth century.
3   The virus of rabies is transmitted through the saliva and salivary glands of animals.
4   Rabies may not develop until eight months or more after infection.
5   The speed with which the disease develops depends partly on the distance of the wound from the brain.
6   One of the stages through which a rabid dog may pass is the inability to move.
7   Pasteur isolated the infective agent from the saliva of a dead rabid animal.
8   The first vaccine experiment on a human being proved to be a failure.
9   A dog gets life-long protection from one powerful injection of the vaccine.
10 If the vaccine is given very soon after a bite from a rabid animal the disease will never develop in human beings.

Vocabulary

Find the following words in the passage and select the meaning you think is *most likely* to correspond among the choices given.

1   *susceptible to* (line 3)
a) suspicious of
b) liable to get
c) resistant to
d) suffering from

2   *ascribed rabies to* (line 4)
a) said rabies was caused by
b) gave rabies to
c) described rabies to
d) restricted rabies to

3   *maniacal* (line 6)
a) mad
b) manly
c) normal
d) medical

4   *provocation* (line 17)
a) sign of fear
b) calling
c) irritation
d) beating

5 *incubation* (line 20)
a) danger
b) development
c) infection
d) paralysed

6 *inevitable* (line 24)
a) inescapable
b) painful
c) quick
d) unenviable

7 *onset* (line 25)
a) beginning
b) disappearance
c) overcoming
d) encouragement

8 *recovered* (line 27)
a) returned
b) cured
c) obtained
d) healed

9 *mortality* (line 39)
a) death
b) disease
c) infection
d) occurrence

10 *circumspectly* (line 45)
a) obviously
b) quickly
c) cautiously
d) round the body

Spot the topic

Choose the phrase or sentence a), b) or c) which most adequately identifies the main point made by the paragraph or paragraphs indicated.

1 *Para. 1* (lines 1–7)
a) General ignorance about rabies today.
b) A scientific account of rabies compared with some historical misconceptions.
c) What happens when a dog gets rabies.

2 *Para. 2* (lines 8–14)
a) Early scientific attempts to control rabies.
b) The clearing of urban centres on the continent.
c) Experiments on the saliva of rabid dogs.

3 *Para. 3* (lines 15–25)
a) A clinical description of rabies in animals.
b) The incubation period of rabies.
c) The effect of rabies on infected dogs.

4 *Para. 4* (lines 26–35)
a) Pasteur and the immunization of dogs against disease.
b) How a boy was once cured of rabies.
c) Pasteur and the development of the rabies vaccine.

5 *Para. 5* (lines 36–45)
a) How rabies was eventually eradicated.
b) The rabies immunization of dogs by vaccination.
c) Vaccine types and the importance of early treatment for humans.

Passage 24

Vitamins

In the early days of sea travel, seamen on long voyages lived exclusively on salted meat and biscuits. Many of them died of scurvy, a disease of the blood which causes swollen gums, livid white spots on the flesh and general exhaustion. On one occasion, in 1535, an English ship arrived in Newfound- land with its crew desperately ill. The men's lives were saved by Iroquois   5 Indians who gave them vegetable leaves to eat. Gradually it came to be realized that scurvy was caused by some lack in the sailors' diet and Captain Cook, on his long voyages of discovery to Australia and New Zealand, established the fact that scurvy could be warded off by the provision of fresh fruit for the sailors.   10

Nowadays it is understood that a diet which contains nothing harmful may yet result in serious disease if certain important elements are missing. These elements are called 'vitamins'. Quite a number of such substances are known and they are given letters to identify them, A, B, C, D, and so on. Different diseases are associated with deficiencies of particular vitamins.   15 Even a slight lack of Vitamin C, for example, the vitamin most plentiful in fresh fruit and vegetables, is thought to increase significantly our susceptibility to colds and influenza.

The vitamins necessary for a healthy body are normally supplied by a good mixed diet, including a variety of fruit and green vegetables. It is   20 only when people try to live on a very restricted diet, say during extended periods of religious fasting, or when trying to lose weight, that it is necessary to make special provision to supply the missing vitamins.

Another example of the dangers of a restricted diet may be seen in the disease known as 'beri-beri, which used to afflict large numbers of Eastern   25 peoples who lived mainly on rice. In the early years of this century, a Dutch scientist called Eijkman was trying to discover the cause of beri- beri. At first he thought it was transmitted by a germ. He was working in a Japanese hospital, where the patients were fed on rice which had had the outer husk* removed from the grain. It was thought this would be easier   30 for weak, sick people to digest.

Eijkman thought his germ theory was confirmed when he noticed the chickens in the hospital yard, which were fed on scraps from the patients' plates, were also showing signs of the disease. He then tried to isolate the germ he thought was causing the disease, but his experiments were   35 interrupted by a hospital official, who decreed that the huskless polished

husk: rougher outer layer.

rice, even though left over by the patients, was too good for chickens. It should be recooked and the chickens fed on cheap, coarse rice with the outer covering still on the grain.

Eijkman noticed that the chickens began to recover on the new diet.   40
He began to consider the possibility that eating unmilled rice somehow prevented or cured beri-beri – even that a lack of some ingredient in the husk might be the cause of the disease. Indeed this was the case. The element needed to prevent beri-beri was shortly afterwards isolated from rice husks and is now known as vitamin B. The milled rice, though more   45
expensive, was in fact perpetuating the disease the hospital was trying to cure. Nowadays, this terrible disease is much less common thanks to our knowledge of vitamins.

Ideas

Select the answer which is most accurate according to the information given in the passage.

1   Scurvy is a disease which causes
a)   loss of blood.
b)   swollen limbs.
c)   exhaustion.
d)   bright red spots on the flesh.

2   Captain Cook
a)   invented vitamins.
b)   established a scurvy factory in Australia.
c)   provided fresh vegetables for his sailors.
d)   warded off attacks on his provisions.

3   A diet which contains nothing harmful
a)   may yet cause scurvy.
b)   has plenty of vitamins.
c)   will usually result in serious disease.
d)   always ensures good health.

4   Deficiencies of the various vitamins
a)   cause identical diseases.
b)   are not serious except in the case of vitamin C.
c)   cause different diseases.
d)   are often caused by scurvy.

5   Fresh fruit and vegetables
a)   contain more vitamin C than any other food.
b)   decrease our resistance to colds.
c)   contain every kind of vitamin.
d)   increase our susceptibility to influenza.

6   A good mixed diet
a)   normally contains enough vitamins.
b)   still needs supplementing with vitamins.
c)   is suitable for religious fasting.
d)   is often difficult to arrange.

7   The disease 'beri-beri'
a)   kills large numbers of western peoples.
b)   is a vitamin deficiency disease.
c)   is transmitted by diseased rice.
d)   can be caught from diseased chickens.

8   The chickens Eijkman noticed in the hospital yard
a)   couldn't digest the huskless rice.
b)   proved beri-beri is transmitted by germs.
c)   were later cooked for the patients' food.
d)   were suffering from vitamin deficiency.

9   Huskless, milled rice
a)   was cheaper than unmilled rice.
b)   was less nourishing than unmilled rice.
c)   was more nourishing than unmilled rice.
d)   cured beri-beri.

10 The ingredient missing from milled rice
a)   was vitamin B.
b)   did not affect the chickens.
c)   was named the Eijkman vitamin.
d)   has never been accurately identified.

Vocabulary

Find the following words in the passage and select the meaning you think is *most likely* to correspond among the choices given.

1   *exclusively* (line 1)
a)   mainly
b)   expensively
c)   entirely
d)   luxuriously

2   *livid* (line 3)
a)   pale
b)   bright red
c)   alive
d)   furious

3   *warded off* (line 9)
a)   kept from hospital wards.
b)   encouraged
c)   avoided
d)   washed off

4   *significantly* (line 17)
a)   quite a lot
b)   symbolically
c)   slightly
d)   momentarily

5 *susceptibility to* (line 18)
a) likelihood of getting
b) resistance to
c) suspicion of
d) liking for

6 *provision* (line 23)
a) food supply
b) containers
c) arrangements
d) omission

7 *isolate* (line 34)
a) keep away
b) prevent
c) separate out
d) avoid

8 *decreed* (line 36)
a) ruled
b) qualified
c) denied
d) legalized

9 *polished* (line 36)
a) rubbed
b) waxed
c) made into flour
d) coloured

10 *perpetuating* (line 46)
a) keeping alive
b) everlasting
c) keeping down
d) changing

Similar or different?

Say whether or not the statement is similar in meaning to the sentence
from the passage indicated by the line number in brackets.

1   Iroquois Indians saved the men's lives by giving them vegetable leaves
    to eat. (lines 5-6)
2   Dietary deficiencies were discovered to result in scurvy, which was
    further established by Captain Cook's successful attempt to counter
    the disease with supplies of fresh fruit. (lines 6-10)
3   Even an apparently harmless diet may be very unhealthy if it is not
    comprehensive enough. (lines 11-12)
4   Even a good mixed diet, with a variety of fruit and green vegetables,
    requires to be supplemented with the necessary vitamins. (lines 19-20)
5   The germ theory of Eijkman was confirmed when chickens, fed on
    scraps from sick patients, became ill also. (lines 32-34)
6   The ingredient required to ward off beri-beri was extracted from rice
    husks and is called vitamin B. (lines 43-45)

Bringing up children (part 1)

It is generally accepted that the experiences of the child in his first years
largely determine his character and later personality. Every experience
teaches the child something and the effects are cumulative. 'Upbringing'
is normally used to refer to the treatment and training of the child within
the home. This is closely related to the treatment and training of the child   5
in school, which is usually distinguished by the term 'education'. In a
society such as ours, both parents and teachers are responsible for the
opportunities provided for the development of the child, so that upbringing and education are interdependent.

The ideals and practices of child rearing vary from culture to culture.   10
In general, the more rural the community, the more uniform are the customs
of child upbringing. In more technologically developed societies, the period
of childhood and adolescence tends to be extended over a long time,
resulting in more opportunity for education and greater variety in
character development.   15

Early upbringing in the home is naturally affected both by the cultural
pattern of the community and by the parents' capabilities and their aims
and depends not only on upbringing and education but also on the innate
abilities of the child. Wide differences of innate intelligence and temperament exist even in children of the same family.   20

Parents can ascertain what is normal in physical, mental and social
development, by referring to some of the many books based on scientific
knowledge in these areas, or, less reliably, since the sample is smaller, by
comparing notes with friends and relatives who have children.

Intelligent parents, however, realize that the particular setting of each   25
family is unique, and there can be no rigid general rules. They use general
information only as a guide in making decisions and solving problems. For
example, they will need specific suggestions for problems such as speech
defects or backwardness in learning to walk or control of bodily functions.
In the more general sense, though, problems of upbringing are recognized   30
to be problems of relationships within the individual family, the first
necessity being a secure emotional background with parents who are united
in their attitude to their children.

All parents have to solve the problems of freedom and discipline. The
younger the child, the more readily the mother gives in to his demands to   35
avoid disappointing him. She knows that if his energies are not given an
outlet, her child's continuing development may be warped. An example
of this is the young child's need to play with mud and sand and water.

Passage 25

A child must be allowed to enjoy this 'messy' but tactile stage of discovery
before he is ready to go on to the less physical pleasures of toys and books. 40
Similarly, throughout life, each stage depends on the satisfactory completion
of the one before.

Ideas

Say whether the following statements are true or false according to the
information given in the passage.

1   An adult's character is in a great measure decided by his childhood
    experiences.
2   Upbringing and education are merely two different words for the same
    process.
3   The way people bring up their children varies throughout the world
    according to differences in culture.
4   Children in more technologically developed societies have stronger
    characters than those from rural communities.
5   Although the cultural pattern of the community affects early up-
    bringing in the home, it is nevertheless not the only factor.
6   Personal contacts tend to be less reliable a method of establishing norms
    of child behaviour than scientific books on the subject.
7   Intelligent parents do not seek outside advice with child problems.
8   Regarding relationships within the family, the first necessity is a secure
    emotional background.
9   If a child were subjected to unusually firm discipline, his development
    might well be adversely affected.
10 The development of the human personality is presented in the passage
    as a series of stages, rather than a smooth progression.

Vocabulary

Find the following words in the passage and select the meaning you think
is *most likely* to correspond among the choices given.

1 *determine* (line 2)
a) decide
b) be positive
c) be determined
d) make up one's mind

2 *are cumulative* (line 3)
a) are dangerous
b) are beneficial
c) become progressively greater
d) immediate

3 *distinguished* (line 6)
a) made honourable
b) defined
c) made famous
d) approved

4 *uniform* (line 11)
a) wearing the same clothes
b) different
c) similar
d) uninformed

5 *innate* (line 19)
a) great
b) unsatisfactory
c) inborn
d) inoperative

6 *ascertain* (line 21)
a) find out
b) bring about
c) assert
d) assure

7 *comparing notes* (line 24)
a) sharing experiences
b) writing down
c) making notes on
d) sharing scientific books

8 *readily* (line 35)
a) prepared
b) quickly
c) doubtfully
d) reluctantly

9 *warped* (line 37)
a) distorted
b) woven
c) speeded up
d) stopped

10 *tactile* (line 39)
a) touching and feeling
b) immature and unnecessary
c) tactical
d) intellectual

Missing word summary

Fill in the numbered blanks from the selection of words given below. The correct choices will complete the sense of this summary of the reading passage.

A child's later character is [1] decided by his early experiences, both at home and in school. Rural communities are [2] more uniform in their child-rearing methods, [3] in the town there is more variety, though early upbringing also depends on the parents' capabilities and the [4] and temperament of the child. [5] parents can get [6] from books or friends on more general points of child [7], they must realize that each home is a unique environment, [8] that questions of freedom and discipline must be considered within each child's individual rate of progress through each stage of development.

1 a) chiefly
  b) entirely
  c) rarely

2 a) seldom
  b) occasionally
  c) usually

3 a) so
  b) while
  c) unless

4 a) co-operation
  b) willingness
  c) intelligence

5 a) While
  b) However
  c) Even

6 a) money
  b) help
  c) scientific knowledge

7 a) psychology
  b) behaviour
  c) health and development

8 a) and
  b) but
  c) except

Passage 26

Bringing up children (part 2)

Where one stage of child development has been left out, or not sufficiently
experienced, the child may have to go back and capture the experience of
it. A good home makes this possible – for example by providing the
opportunity for the child to play with a clockwork car or toy railway
train up to any age if he still needs to do so. This principle, in fact, under-   5
lies all psychological treatment of children in difficulties with their
development, and is the basis of work in child clinics.

The beginnings of discipline are in the nursery. Even the youngest baby
is taught by gradual stages to wait for food, to sleep and wake at regular
intervals and so on. If the child feels the world around him is a warm and   10
friendly one, he slowly accepts its rhythm and accustoms himself to
conforming to its demands. Learning to wait for things, particularly for
food, is a very important element in upbringing, and is achieved successfully only if too great demands are not made before the child can understand them.   15

Every parent watches eagerly the child's acquisition of each new skill –
the first spoken words, the first independent steps, or the beginning of
reading and writing. It is often tempting to hurry the child beyond his
natural learning rate, but this can set up dangerous feelings of failure and
states of anxiety in the child. This might happen at any stage. A baby   20
might be forced to use a toilet too early, a young child might be encouraged
to learn to read before he knows the meaning of the words he reads. On
the other hand, though, if a child is left alone too much, or without any
learning opportunities, he loses his natural zest for life and his desire to
find out new things for himself.   25

Learning together is a fruitful source of relationship between children
and parents. By playing together, parents learn more about their children
and children learn more from their parents. Toys and games which both
parents and children can share are an important means of achieving this
co-operation. Building-block toys, jigsaw* puzzles and crosswords* are   30
good examples.

Parents vary greatly in their degree of strictness or indulgence towards
their children. Some may be especially strict in money matters, others are
severe over times of coming home at night, punctuality for meals or

* *jigsaw:* a puzzle in which irregularly shaped, cut-out pieces must be fitted together to form a
complete picture.
* *crossword:* a form of puzzle often found in newspapers in which a pattern of blank squares is
filled in with words guessed from a set of clues containing hidden meanings.

personal cleanliness. In general, the controls imposed represent the needs 35
of the parents and the values of the community as much as the child's own
happiness and well-being.

As regards the development of *moral* standards in the growing child,
consistency is very important in parental teaching. To forbid a thing one
day and excuse it the next is no foundation for morality. Also, parents 40
should realize that 'example is better than precept'. If they are hypo-
critical and do not practise what they preach, their children may grow
confused and emotionally insecure when they grow old enough to think
for themselves, and realize they have been to some extent deceived. A
sudden awareness of a marked difference between their parents' ethics and 45
their morals can be a dangerous disillusion.

Ideas

Select the answer which is most accurate according to the information given
in the passage.

1 The principle underlying all treatment of developmental difficulties
   in children
a) is in the provision of clockwork toys and trains.
b) offers recapture of earlier experiences.
c) is to send them to clinics.
d) is to capture them before they are sufficiently experienced.

2 The child in the nursery
a) doesn't initially sleep and wake at regular intervals.
b) quickly learns to wait for food.
c) always accepts the rhythm of the world around him.
d) always feels the world around him is warm and friendly.

3 Learning to wait for things is successfully taught
a) only if excessive demands are avoided.
b) in spite of excessive demands being made.
c) because excessive demands are not advisable.
d) is achieved successfully by all children.

4 Eagerly watching the child's acquisition of new skills
a) should be avoided.
b) sets up dangerous states of anxiety.
c) is universal among parents.
d) is characteristic of materially developed societies.

5 The encouragement of children to achieve new skills
a) should be left to schoolteachers.
b) can never be taken too far.
c) will always assist their development.
d) should be balanced between the extremes of pushing and lack of
    interest.

6   By playing together
a)   children teach their parents more.
b)   parents learn more about the world from their children.
c)   parents tend to become like their children.
d)   parents and children learn from each other.

7   Jigsaw puzzles are
a)   too difficult for children.
b)   a kind of building-block toy.
c)   a suitable exercise for parent–child co-operation.
d)   not very entertaining for adults.

8   Parental controls and discipline
a)   are designed to promote the child's happiness.
b)   serve a dual purpose.
c)   reflect only the needs of the parents and the values of the community.
d)   should be avoided as far as possible.

9   As regards rules, parents should
a)   make as few exceptions as possible.
b)   vary the discipline according to circumstance.
c)   be harsh in their punishments.
d)   discontinue rules their children dislike.

10 'Example is better than precept'
a)   doesn't work when the children grow old enough to think for them-
     selves.
b)   is a rule which ensures a child will not be disillusioned when he grows
     up.
c)   because it avoids the necessity for ethics and morals.
d)   is an impossible rule for most parents.

Vocabulary

Find the following words in the passage and select the meaning you think
is *most likely* to correspond among the choices given.

1   *train* (line 5)
a)   sequence
b)   discipline
c)   exercise
d)   vehicle

2   *underlies* (line 5)
a)   is the basis of
b)   gives the lie to
c)   understates
d)   undermines

3   *conforming to* (line 12)
a)   reforming
b)   adapting to
c)   confronted with
d)   reshaping

4   *zest* (line 24)
a)   enthusiasm
b)   aptitude
c)   intelligence
d)   feelings

5   *imposed* (line 35)
a) stamped
b) pressed
c) forcibly applied
d) inconvenienced

6   *consistency* (line 39)
a) quality
b) sameness
c) strictness
d) character

7   *precept* (line 41)
a) cure
b) punishment
c) instruction
d) prevention

8   *marked* (line 45)
a) obvious
b) praised
c) corrected
d) spoiled

9   *ethics* (line 45)
a) behaviour
b) principles
c) instructions
d) ideas

10 *morals* (line 46)
a) behaviour
b) principles
c) instructions
d) ideas

Spot the topic

Choose the phrase or sentence a), b) or c) which most adequately identifies
the main point made by the paragraph or paragraphs indicated.

1   *Para. 2* (lines 8–15)
a) The baby's life in the nursery.
b) Learning to wait for food.
c) The gradual process of learning discipline.

2   *Para. 3* (lines 16–25)
a) The delicate balance between parental support and excessive interference.
b) How parents eagerly watch their children's development.
c) The dangers of leaving a child alone too much.

3   *Para. 5* (lines 32–37)
a) Parents must be strict with their children.
b) Parental restrictions vary, and are not always enforced for the child's
    benefit alone.
c) Parental rules should include punctuality for meals and personal
    cleanliness.

4   *Para. 6* (lines 38–46)
a) In moral matters, parents should be strict and should also try to keep to
    the rules themselves.
b) In moral matters, parents should be aware of the marked differences
    between adults and children.
c) Simply forbidding things is not a good foundation for morality.

Discussion

Questions for class discussion, and/or brief written answers.

1   Do you think parents are justified in disciplining their children merely in order to make their own lives more comfortable?

2   Are there any other factors that might affect the development of a child apart from parental teaching, education and innate inability?

3   Which do you think is more important for success in life – innate ability or wealth and social position? Can you think of examples and counter-examples from your own experience or from history? What do *you* think 'success in life' really means?

4   Do you think yourself that a child should be allowed to play with mud, water, sand or any other messy or dirty substance until he 'grows out of it'? Were you allowed to as a child?

5   As a child or adolescent, did *you* find any discrepancy between what your elders and parents *told* you to do, and the way they behaved them- selves? If so, can you remember examples? Were you ever at all disillusioned?

6   There is a widely held belief that poverty, hardship and deprivation produce incentive to achieve. 'The best fighter is a hungry fighter' is a maxim of the boxing world, and there is a popular romantic stereo- type of the artist or writer of genius, 'starving in a garret'. How do you reconcile this with the passage which suggests that the child should ideally be made to feel 'that the world around him is a warm and friendly place'?

7   What is your opinion of modern child psychology as opposed to folk wisdom and personal experience in bringing up children? Can you think of examples to support your view from what you have read or experienced?

8   Do you think you had enough or too much encouragement to succeed in childhood and early adolescence (part 2, para. 3)? Can you think of examples?

9   Do you remember playing together with your parents or older relatives? Do you think children *need* to be treated in this way?

10 'Spare the rod and spoil the child.' How far do you agree with this old English proverb?

Etiquette (part 1)

The origins of etiquette 'the conventional rules of behaviour and ceremonies
observed in polite society' are complex. One of them is respect for authority.
From the most primitive times, subjects showed respect for their ruler by
bowing, prostrating themselves on the ground, not speaking until spoken to,
and never turning their backs to the throne. Some monarchs developed   5
rules to stress even further the respect due to them. The emperors of
Byzantium expected their subjects to kiss their feet. When an ambassador
from abroad was introduced, he had to touch the ground before the throne
with his forehead. Meanwhile the throne itself was raised in the air so that,
on looking up, the ambassador saw the ruler far above him, haughty and   10
remote.

    Absolute rulers have, as a rule, made etiquette more complicated rather
than simpler. The purpose is not only to make the ruler seem almost god-
like, but also to protect him from familiarity, for without some such
protection his life, lived inevitably in the public eye, would be intolerable.   15
The court of Louis XIV of France provided an excellent example of a
very highly developed system of etiquette. Because the king and his family
were considered to belong to France, they were almost continually on
show among their courtiers. They woke, prayed, washed and dressed before
crowds of courtiers. Even larger crowds watched them eat their meals, and   20
access to their palaces was free to all their subjects.

    Yet this public life was organized so minutely, with such a refinement
of ceremonial, that the authority of the King and the respect in which he
was held grew steadily throughout his lifetime. A crowd watched him
dress, but only the Duke who was his first *valet de chambre* was allowed   25
to hold out the right sleeve of his shirt, only the Prince who was his Grand
Chamberlain could relieve him of his dressing gown, and only the Master
of the Wardrobe might help him pull up his breeches. These were not
familiarities, nor merely duties, but highly coveted privileges. Napoleon
recognized the value of ceremony to a ruler. When he became Emperor, he   30
discarded the Revolutionary custom of calling everyone 'citizen', restored
much of the Court ceremonial that the Revolution had destroyed, and
recalled members of the nobility to instruct his new court in the old formal
manners.

    Rules of etiquette may prevent embarrassment and even serious disputes. 35
The general rule of social precedence is that people of greater importance
precede those of lesser importance. Before the rules of diplomatic
precedence were worked out in the early sixteenth century, rival ambassa-

dors often fought for the most honourable seating position at a function. Before the principle was established that ambassadors of various countries should sign treaties in order of seniority, disputes arose as to who should sign first. The establishment of rules for such matters prevented uncertainty and disagreement, as do rules for less important occasions. For example, at an English wedding, the mother of the bridegroom should sit in the first pew or bench on the right-hand side of the church. The result is dignity and order.　45

Outside palace circles, the main concern of etiquette has been to make harmonious the behaviour of equals, but sometimes social classes have used etiquette as a weapon against intruders, refining their manners in order to mark themselves off from the lower class.　50

Ideas

Say whether the following statements are true or false according to the information given in the passage.

1 The origins of etiquette are based simply on respect for authority.
2 The emperors of Byzantium went to considerable lengths to stress the respect due to them.
3 Absolute rulers have, as a rule, found life in the public eye intolerable.
4 It was difficult for ordinary people to catch a glimpse of Louis XIV of France.
5 A large crowd of people used to gather round Louis XIV when he dressed, struggling for the honour of assisting him with his various pieces of clothing.
6 Napoleon discarded aristocratic privileges when he became Emperor of France.
7 Embarrassment and even serious disputes may be caused by want of etiquette.
8 Before the sixteenth century, fights between ambassadors over precedence were not uncommon.
9 At an English wedding, the bride's mother has to sit in the first pew or bench on the right-hand side of the church.
10 Etiquette is not always used to make life easier for people.

Vocabulary

Find the following words in the passage and select the meaning you think is *most likely* to correspond among the choices given.

1 *subjects* (line 3)
a) controls
b) citizens
c) topics
d) school studies

2 *prostrating themselves* (line 4)
a) lying flat
b) keeping silent
c) facing the throne
d) bending the knee

3 *stress* (line 6)
a) strain
b) difficulty
c) emphasize
d) suffer

4 *on show* (lines 18–19)
a) in public view
b) at the theatre
c) being exhibited for money
d) raised on a platform

5 *access to* (line 21)
a) food and drink
b) a view of
c) admittance to
d) entrance ticket to

6 *so minutely* (line 22)
a) every minute
b) so quickly
c) in such detail
d) timed to the exact minute

7 *coveted* (line 29)
a) desired
b) hidden
c) unpleasant
d) secret

8 *discarded* (line 31)
a) revived
b) rejected
c) supported
d) discussed

9 *recalled* (line 33)
a) remembered
b) renamed
c) invited back
d) refused

10 *worked out* (line 38)
a) drawn up
b) outdated
c) removed
d) ceased to be useful

Similar or different?

Say whether or not the statement is similar in meaning to the sentence from the passage indicated by the line number in brackets.

1 The more absolute the authority of the ruler, the more etiquette has tended towards elaboration. (lines 12–13)
2 The King and his family used to travel about France as if they owned it, giving elaborate theatrical performances. (lines 17–19)
3 Though many people watched him dress, each item of clothing was the particular concern of a designated individual. (lines 24–28)
4 He was not unwilling, when he became Emperor, to discard Court ceremonial, and instruct recalled members of the nobility in Revolutionary procedures. (lines 30–34)
5 Uncertainty and discord led to the establishment of rules, including rules for lesser occasions. (lines 42–43)
6 Outside palace circles, the separation of social classes has been the principal purpose of etiquette. (lines 47–50)

Etiquette (part 2)

In sixteenth-century Italy and eighteenth-century France, waning
prosperity and increasing social unrest led the ruling families to try to
preserve their superiority by withdrawing from the lower and middle
classes behind barriers of etiquette. In a prosperous community, on the
other hand, polite society soon absorbs the newly rich, and in England   5
there has never been any shortage of books on etiquette for teaching them
the manners appropriate to their new way of life.

Every code of etiquette has contained three elements: basic moral duties;
practical rules which promote efficiency; and artificial, optional graces such
as formal compliments to, say, women on their beauty or superiors on their   10
generosity and importance.

In the first category are consideration for the weak and respect for age.
Among the ancient Egyptians the young always stood in the presence of
older people. Among the Mponguwe of Tanzania, the young men bow as
they pass the huts of the elders. In England, until about a century ago,   15
young children did not sit in their parents' presence without asking permission.

Practical rules are helpful in such ordinary occurrences of social life
as making proper introductions at parties or other functions so that people
can be brought to know each other. Before the invention of the fork,   20
etiquette directed that the fingers should be kept as clean as possible;
before the handkerchief came into common use, etiquette suggested that,
after spitting, a person should rub the spit inconspicuously underfoot.

Extremely refined behaviour, however, cultivated as an art of gracious
living, has been characteristic only of societies with wealth and leisure,   25
which admitted women as the social equals of men. After the fall of Rome,
the first European society to regulate behaviour in private life in accordance
with a complicated code of etiquette was twelfth-century Provence, in
France.

Provence had become wealthy. The lords had returned to their castles   30
from the crusades, and there the ideals of chivalry grew up, which emphasized the virtue and gentleness of women and demanded that a knight
should profess a pure and dedicated love to a lady who would be his
inspiration, and to whom he would dedicate his valiant deeds, though he
would never come physically close to her. This was the introduction of the   35
concept of romantic love, which was to influence literature for many
hundreds of years and which still lives on in a debased form in simple
popular songs and cheap novels today.

In Renaissance Italy too, in the fourteenth and fifteenth centuries, a wealthy and leisured society developed an extremely complex code of manners, but the rules of behaviour of fashionable society had little influence on the daily life of the lower classes. Indeed many of the rules, such as how to enter a banquet room, or how to use a sword or handkerchief for ceremonial purposes, were irrelevant to the way of life of the average working man, who spent most of his life outdoors or in his own poor hut and most probably did not have a handkerchief, certainly not a sword, to his name. 40 45

Yet the essential basis of all good manners does not vary. Consideration for the old and weak and the avoidance of harming or giving unnecessary offence to others is a feature of all societies everywhere and at all levels from the highest to the lowest. You can easily think of dozens of examples of customs and habits in your own daily life which come under this heading. 50

Ideas

Select the answer which is most accurate according to the information given in the passage.

1 In sixteenth-century Italy and eighteenth-century France, the ruling families
a) tried to destroy the lower and middle classes using etiquette.
b) discriminated against the lower classes using etiquette.
c) tried to teach etiquette to the lower and middle classes.
d) put the middle and working classes into fenced enclosures.

2 In England, the upper classes
a) have always followed the French attitude to the lower classes.
b) accept the newly rich in spite of their lower-class manners.
c) publish books on etiquette for the newly rich.
d) seem to accept a newly rich person provided he makes some attempt to adjust to upper-class life.

3 Every code of etiquette has contained three elements:
a) practical rules, optional moral duties and formal compliments.
b) formal compliments, basic moral duties and practical rules.
c) optional moral duties, optional practical rules and artificial graces.
d) rules, regulations and requirements.

4 The custom of young men bowing to show respect when passing the dwellings of their elders was cited as a characteristic of
a) the ancient Egyptians.
b) parts of Tanzania.
c) England, about a century ago.
d) all societies.

5   The practical rules of etiquette, for example those governing table manners
a)   are the same all over the world.
b)   sometimes vary according to time and circumstance.
c)   became unnecessary with the invention of the knife and fork.
d)   are not liable to change.

6   Etiquette cultivated as an art of gracious living
a)   has been typical of rich and leisured societies.
b)   advocates that women are the same as men.
c)   began in nineteenth-century Provence.
d)   looks down on extremely refined behaviour.

7   The ideals of chivalry demanded that
a)   a knight should never have physical relationships with women.
b)   a knight should inspire his lady to valiant deeds.
c)   a knight should dedicate his valiant deeds to a woman.
d)   romantic people should influence literature.

8   The rules of etiquette in Renaissance Italy
a)   were chiefly concerned with the correct use of one's sword or handkerchief.
b)   were practised by the majority of society.
c)   did not apply to a large section of society.
d)   were fairly simple to follow.

9   The average working man in fifteenth-century Italy
a)   spent all his life outdoors.
b)   spent all his life in his own poor hut.
c)   had better social manners than workers today.
d)   was unlikely to have possessed a sword.

10 Consideration for the old and weak and the avoidance of giving unnecessary offence to others are
a)   the essential basis of all systems of good manners.
b)   not a universal feature of etiquette.
c)   taught to the lower classes by the upper classes.
d)   often neglected by polite society.

Vocabulary

Find the following words in the passage and select the meaning you think is *most likely* to correspond among the choices given.

1   *waning* (line 1)
a)   increasing
b)   steady
c)   declining
d)   winning

2   *absorbs* (line 5)
a)   accepts
b)   interests
c)   is interested by
d)   dries up

3 *appropriate to* (line 7)
a) in keeping with
b) stealing from
c) unsuitable for
d) opposite from

4 *inconspicuously* (line 23)
a) vigorously
b) carefully
c) unobtrusively
d) unconsciously

5 *characteristic* (line 25)
a) possible
b) typical
c) interesting
d) morally good

6 *admitted* (line 26)
a) accepted
b) contributed
c) confessed
d) agreed

7 *concept* (line 36)
a) deception
b) mistake
c) idea
d) beginning

8 *debased* (line 37)
a) inferior
b) developed
c) insecure
d) lacking foundation

9 *irrelevant to* (line 44)
a) insulting to
b) not applicable to
c) hostile to
d) related to

10 *feature* (line 50)
a) face
b) defect
c) variation
d) characteristic

Missing word summary

Fill in the numbered blanks from the selection of words given below. The correct choices will complete the sense of this summary of the reading passage.

While declining societies used etiquette as a [1] between classes, prosperous countries such as England were quite willing to allow successful people from the lower classes to move up in [2]. They had to learn the three elements of good manners [3], the basic moral duties, the [4] rules and optional graces [5] compliments to women or superiors. The old and weak have always been respected in codes of etiquette, and the practical rules help us to live together without [6] others. [7] in spite of the over-elaborate codes, [8], that which arose in twelfth-century Provence, the essential basis of good manners, concern for the old and weak, and the avoidance of offending others unnecessarily, does not vary.

1 a) leveller
   b) barrier
   c) bridge

2 a) wealth
   b) skill
   c) society

3 a) except
   b) namely
   c) also

4 a) practical
   b) difficult
   c) complimentary

5	a) in addition		7	a) Yet
	b) such as			b) Although
	c) except for			c) Not
6	a) helping		8	a) for instance
	b) teaching			b) not like
	c) annoying			c) apart from

Discussion topics

Questions for class discussion, and/or brief written answers.

1   Can you add any more examples of old customs of politeness and ceremony similar to those mentioned in the two passages?
2   The actual words we use (e.g. forms of address) also show respect or the opposite. What examples can you think of in your language? Is this closely connected with class distinctions?
3   Does the English language have its own ways of showing respect or the opposite? Can you think of different degrees of politeness for saying the same thing (e.g. ' sit down')?
4   Are there aspects of behaviour which seem to be acceptable among foreigners which are considered impolite in your society?
5   Are there customs accepted in your society which foreigners find unusual?
6   Is what is polite or acceptable in one region of your country considered in the same way elsewhere?
7   Is the older generation more concerned with what is polite than the younger generation? If so, why?
8   Do young people develop their own codes of acceptable behaviour? If so, give examples and consider why this may be.
9   What do you think the saying ' Manners makyth man' means? Has it any deep value?

Passage 29

Social classes (part 1)

It is hard to get any agreement on the precise meaning of the term 'social class'. In everyday life, people tend to have a different approach to those they consider their equals from that which they assume with people they consider higher or lower than themselves in the social scale. The criteria we use to 'place' a new acquaintance, however, are a complex mixture   5
of factors. Dress, way of speaking, area of residence in a given city or province, education and manners all play a part.

In ancient civilizations, the Sumerian, for example, which flourished in the lower Euphrates valley from 2000 to 5000 B.C. social differences were based on birth, status or rank, rather than on wealth. Four main classes   10
were recognized. These were the rulers, the priestly administrators, the freemen (such as craftsmen, merchants or farmers) and the slaves.

In Greece, after the sixth-century B.C., there was a growing conflict between the peasants and the landed aristocrats,* and a gradual decrease in the power of the aristocracy when a kind of 'middle class' of traders and   15
skilled workers grew up. The population of Athens, for example, was divided into three main classes which were politically and legally distinct. About one-third of the total were slaves, who did not count politically at all, a fact often forgotten by those who praise Athens as the nursery of democracy. The next main group consisted of resident foreigners, the   20
'metics', who were freemen, though they too were allowed no share in political life. The third group was the powerful body of 'citizens', who were themselves divided into sub-classes.

In ancient Rome, too, a similar struggle between the *plebs,* or working people, and the landed families was a recurrent feature of social life.   25

The medieval feudal system, which flourished in Europe from the ninth to the thirteenth centuries, gave rise to a comparatively simple system based on birth. Under the king there were two main classes – lords and 'vassals', the latter with many subdivisions. The vassal owed the lord fidelity, obedience and aid, especially in the form of military service. The   30
lord in return owed his vassal protection and an assured livelihood.

In the later Middle Ages, however, the development of a money economy and the growth of cities and trade led to the rise of another class, the 'burghers' or city merchants and mayors. These were the predecessors of the modern middle classes. Gradually high office and occupation assumed   35
importance in determining social position, as it became more and more

* *landed aristocrats:* land-owning noblemen.

108

possible for a person born to one station in life to move to another. This change affected the towns more than the country areas, where remnants of feudalism lasted much longer.

With the break-up of the feudal economy, the increasing division of labour, and the growing power of the town burghers, the commercial and professional middle class became more and more important in Europe, and the older privileged class, the landed aristocracy, began to lose some of its power.

40

Ideas

Select the answer which is most accurate according to the information given in the passage.

1 We 'place' people in society in relation to ourselves
a) because we dislike them.
b) because we feel superior to them.
c) mainly by their dress.
d) according to a complex mixture of factors.

2 We evaluate other people's social position by
a) questioning them in great detail.
b) their dress, manners, area of residence and other factors.
c) finding out how much their salary is.
d) the kind of job they do.

3 The four main classes of Sumerian civilization
a) did not include slaves.
b) took little account of financial standing.
c) took little account of status or rank.
d) were not clearly defined.

4 The decline of the Greek aristocracy's power in the sixth century B.C.
a) caused international conflicts in the area.
b) coincided with the rise of a new 'middle class' of traders and peasants.
c) was assisted by a rise in the number of slaves.
d) lasted for only a short time.

5 Slaves in Greece in the sixth century B.C.
a) were not allowed to count votes at elections.
b) were kept ignorant as a political measure.
c) were not politically significant.
d) controlled one-third of the democratic vote.

6 Athens is often praised as the nursery of democracy
a) even though slaves were allowed to vote.
b) because its three main classes were politically and legally distinct.

c) in spite of its heavy dependence on slave labour.
d) because even very young children could vote.

7   Under the medieval feudal system
a) there were four main divisions.
b) the lords mercilessly exploited the vassals.
c) the lords had certain duties towards their peasants.
d) the vassals often fought against the lords.

8   Medieval lords recruited their armies
a) from among their peasants.
b) from among the freemen.
c) by offering the soldiers high rates of pay.
d) in order to get an assured livelihood.

9   The 'burghers' of the later Middle Ages
a) became more powerful than the old aristocracy.
b) ignored class distinctions.
c) created an entirely new social class.
d) were mainly to be found in country areas.

10 The rise of the commercial and professional middle class
a) was predominantly an urban, as opposed to a rural phenomenon.
b) predated the establishment of the feudal system.
c) had little effect on the feudal system.
d) was bitterly opposed by the feudal lords.

Vocabulary

Find the following words in the passage and select the meaning you think
is *most likely* to correspond among the choices given.

1   *assume* (line 3)
a) guess
b) use
c) disguise
d) imagine

2   *criteria* (line 4)
a) characteristics
b) words
c) standards of judgement
d) criticisms

3   *count* (line 18)
a) have importance
b) add
c) calculate
d) total

4   *recurrent* (line 25)
a) rare
b) powerful
c) re-occurring
d) electrical

5   *predecessors* (line 34)
a) supporters
b) descendants
c) ancestors
d) most important

6   *office* (line 35)
a) work room
b) wealth
c) office work
d) official position

7 *occupation* (line 35)
a) profession
b) space occupied
c) taking over
d) invasion

8 *station* (line 37)
a) stopping place
b) goal
c) village
d) social rank

9 *remnants* (line 38)
a) remains
b) opponents
c) torn clothing
d) garments

10 *landed* (line 43)
a) stranded
b) isolated
c) having land
d) tenant

Spot the topic

Choose the phrase or sentence a), b) or c) which most adequately identifies the main point made by the paragraph or paragraphs indicated.

1 *Para. 1* (lines 1–7)
a) Evaluating a person's social class is a very complex procedure.
b) A person will vary his social class in everyday life.
c) Guessing a person's social class by his clothes and the way he speaks.

2 *Para. 2* (lines 8–12)
a) Social differences based on birth and wealth in the ancient world.
b) Sumeria had both ruler and priestly administrators.
c) The four classes of ancient Sumerian society.

3 *Para. 3* (lines 13–23)
a) The struggle of the Greek peasants in the fifth century B.C.
b) The class structure of Ancient Greece.
c) The slave economy of Athens.

4 *Para. 5* (lines 26–31)
a) The two main classes of the medieval feudal system.
b) The relationship between the king and his vassals from the ninth to the thirteenth centuries.
c) The obligations of the medieval vassal.

5 *Para. 6* (lines 32–39)
a) The money economy and the growth of trade in the Middle Ages.
b) The remnants of feudalism in the countryside of the Middle Ages.
c) Social mobility through trade in the later Middle Ages.

Passage 30

Social classes (part 2)

In the eighteenth-century one of the first modern economists, Adam Smith, thought that the 'whole annual produce of the land and labour of every country' provided revenue to 'three different orders of people: those who live by rent, those who live by wages, and those who live by profit'. Each successive stage of the industrial revolution, however, made the social   5
structure more complicated.

Many intermediate groups grew up during the nineteenth-century between the upper middle class and the working class. There were small-scale industrialists as well as large ones, small shopkeepers and tradesmen, officials and salaried employees, skilled and unskilled workers, and   10
professional men such as doctors and teachers. Farmers and peasants continued in all countries as independent groups.

In spite of this development, one of the most famous writers on social class in the nineteenth century, Karl Marx, thought that there was a tendency for society to split up into huge class camps, the bourgeoisie   15
(the capitalists) and the proletariat (the workers). Influential as was Marx's theory of social class, it was much over-simplified. The social make-up of modern societies is much more complex than he suggested.

During the nineteenth and early twentieth centuries the possession of wealth inevitably affected a person's social position. Intelligent industrialists 20
with initiative made fortunes by their wits which lifted them into an eco-nomic group far higher than that of their working-class parents. But they lacked the social training of the upper class, who despised them as the 'new rich'.

They often sent their sons and daughters to special schools to acquire   25
social training. Here their children mixed with the children of the upper classes, were accepted by them, and very often found marriage partners from among them. In the same way, a thrifty, hardworking labourer, though not clever himself, might save for his son enough to pay for an extended secondary school education in the hope that he would move into a 'white-   30
collar' occupation, carrying with it a higher salary and a move up in the social scale.

The tendency to move down in social class is less obvious, for a claim to an aristocratic birth, especially in Europe, has always carried a certain distinction, and people have made tremendous efforts to obtain for their   35
children the kind of opportunities they had for themselves.

In the twentieth century the increased taxation of higher incomes, the growth of the social services, and the wider development of educa-

tional opportunity have considerably altered the social outlook. The
upper classes no longer are the sole, or even the main possessors of wealth,   40
power and education, though inherited social position still carries considerable prestige.

Many people today are hostile towards class distinctions and privileges
and hope to achieve a classless society. The trouble is that as one inequality
is removed, another tends to take its place, and the best that has so far   45
been attempted is a society in which distinctions are elastic and in which
every member has fair opportunities for making the best of his abilities.

Ideas

Select the answer which is most accurate according to the information given
in the passage.

1   Adam Smith's eighteenth-century definition of class was invalidated by
a)   Karl Marx.
b)   the nineteenth-century working class.
c)   the social influence of farmers and peasants.
d)   successive stages of the industrial revolution.

2   During the nineteenth century, many intermediate groups grew up
a)   between the upper class and the middle class.
b)   between the working class and the upper middle class.
c)   within the working class.
d)   within the aristocracy.

3   The writer regards doctors and teachers as
a)   middle class.
b)   working class.
c)   upper class.
d)   independent groups outside society.

4   Karl Marx developed his two-class theory
a)   in spite of the farmers and peasants.
b)   even though new sub-classes were appearing in his day.
c)   making special allowance for doctors and salaried employees.
d)   with reference to European societies only.

5   Marx's theory of social class was
a)   oversimplified by the bourgeoisie.
b)   influential because it was oversimplified.
c)   influential in spite of being oversimplified.
d)   not widely known in the nineteenth century.

6   The ' new rich '
a)   often married into the upper class.
b)   despised the upper class.

c) were often men of initiative and intelligence.
d) seldom allowed their children to mix with the upper class.

7   The children of the 'new rich'
a) were accepted by the upper class because of their education.
b) were accepted by the upper class in spite of their education.
c) despised their parents.
d) secretly hated the aristocracy.

8   A 'white-collar' occupation
a) is mainly suitable for labourers.
b) is an upper-class occupation.
c) represents social advance for a labourer's son.
d) was regarded as unmanly by the labouring class in the nineteenth century.

9   In the twentieth century class differences have been partly smoothed
    out by
a) decreased taxation.
b) taxation, social services and education.
c) education, women's rights and industrial development.
d) government enforcement of equal rights.

10 Though a classless society has yet to be perfected, an attempt *has* been
    made to provide
a) equal opportunity.
b) equal rights.
c) equal classes numerically.
d) equal pay for all workers.

Vocabulary

Find the following words in the passage and select the meaning you think
is *most likely* to correspond among the choices given.

1   *orders* (line 3)
a) commands
b) officials
c) regulations
d) groups

c) uncertain
d) vague

2   *successive* (line 5)
a) successful
b) following
c) increasing
d) yearly

4   *camps* (line 15)
a) villages
b) holiday accommodation
c) tent sites
d) sections

5   *make-up* (line 17)
a) composition
b) progress
c) disguise
d) cosmetics

3   *intermediate* (line 7)
a) in between
b) of average difficulty

6 *initiative* (line 21)
a) intelligence
b) hard work
c) originality of thought
d) financial resources

7 *thrifty* (line 28)
a) cunning
b) careful with money
c) quick-witted
d) thirsty

8 *'white-collar' occupation* (lines 30-31)
a) working as a tailor
b) working in a laundry

c) working in an office
d) being a priest

9 *obvious* (line 33)
a) clearly argued
b) clearly stated
c) clearly observed
d) avoided

10 *elastic* (line 46)
a) made of rubber
b) tightly constricting
c) long lasting
d) not too rigid

Similar or different?

Say whether or not the statement is similar in meaning to the sentence from the passage indicated by the line number in brackets.

1 The structure of society became less clear-cut as the industrial revolution proceeded. (lines 4-6)
2 All over the world, farmers and peasants continued the struggle to attain their independence. (lines 11-12)
3 Marx's theory of social class was oversimplified so that it would become influential. (lines 16-17)
4 Industrialists who became successful and rich in the nineteenth and early twentieth centuries could not avoid changing their social class. (lines 20-22)
5 The newly rich were despised by the upper class, whose social training they lacked. (lines 22-24)
6 Similarly, the labourer might hope to move into a 'white-collar' occupation with a higher salary and improved status thanks to the extended secondary-school education of his son. (lines 28-32)
7 A society without classes is the goal today of many people who are against class barriers. (lines 43-44)

Discussion topics

Questions for class discussion and/or brief written answers.

1 Why is a simple three-stage division of society such as Adam Smith's too oversimplified for the modern world? (or is this 'begging the question'?)
2 What factors do you think might lead farmers and peasants to remain 'independent groups' in modern society? What factors might make them less isolated in future?

3   Do you think Karl Marx's view of society as two opposed camps is justified in your experience? What effect do you think education might have on Marx's 'proletariat' – or the development of small businesses?

4   What sort of problems, in detail, do you think one of the 'new rich' might have – especially in his social and private life?

5   What sort of things did the sons and daughters of the 'new rich' hope to get from an education at an expensive school?

6   How has education affected your own social status, if at all? Do you think it will in future?

7   Do you think education, and an eventual 'white-collar' job might create problems between a poor student and his family? If so, give examples.

8   What sort of things do you think might bring a man down in social class? Do you know any examples of people who have 'come down in the world' in this way?

9   What factors have tended to reduce class barriers in the twentieth century?

10 Do you think human nature would ever allow the evolution of a 'classless' society? What measures do you think would help a move towards such a state?

Answers

Introductory passage 1: *Faster effective reading*
Ideas: 1a, 2b, 3a, 4d, 5b, 6b, 7a, 8c, 9b, 10d
Vocabulary: 1a, 2d, 3b, 4a, 5a, 6c, 7b, 8a, 9b, 10c
Spot the topic: 1b, 2c, 3b, 4a, 5a

Introductory passage 2: *Some obstacles to faster effective reading*
Ideas: 1t, 2f, 3t, 4t, 5t, 6f, 7t, 8f, 9f, 10f
Vocabulary: 1d, 2a, 3c, 4c, 5a, 6c, 7a, 8b, 9c, 10a
Missing word summary: 1b, 2a, 3b, 4c, 5c, 6b, 7a

Introductory passage 3: *Practical hints for reading practice (1)*
Ideas: 1c, 2b, 3d, 4a, 5c, 6b, 7a, 8c, 9b, 10a
Vocabulary: 1b, 2d, 3a, 4b, 5c, 6a, 7c, 8a, 9c, 10c
Similar or different?: 1d, 2s, 3s, 4d, 5s, 6d

Introductory passage 4: *Practical hints for reading practice (2)*
Ideas: 1b, 2b, 3a, 4a, 5c, 6b, 7c, 8b, 9a, 10d
Vocabulary: 1i, 2f, 3g, 4j, 5k, 6l, 7d, 8e, 9c, 10b
Spot the topic: 1b, 2c, 3b, 4c, 5b

Passage 5: *Money*
Ideas: 1b, 2a, 3d, 4b, 5c, 6a, 7a, 8b, 9c, 10d
Vocabulary: 1a, 2a, 3c, 4a, 5b, 6a, 7d, 8b, 9c, 10a
Missing word summary: 1c, 2c, 3b, 4b, 5c, 6a, 7c, 8a

Passage 6: *Diamonds*
Ideas: 1c, 2d, 3b, 4b, 5c, 6a, 7c, 8d, 9b, 10a
Vocabulary: 1c, 2b, 3a, 4b, 5c, 6a, 7b, 8a, 9a, 10c
Missing word summary: 1c, 2b, 3a, 4b, 5b, 6b, 7a, 8a

Passage 7: *Canning food*
Ideas: 1f, 2t, 3f, 4f, 5t, 6f, 7f, 8t, 9f, 10f
Vocabulary: 1d, 2b, 3a, 4b, 5c, 6a, 7a, 8b, 9c, 10a
Spot the topic: 1a, 2a, 3c, 4b, 5baedfc (1b, 2a, 3e, 4d, 5f, 6c)

Passage 8: *The Olympic Games*
Ideas: 1b, 2b, 3a, 4d, 5b, 6a, 7c, 8a, 9b, 10a
Vocabulary: 1c, 2a, 3b, 4a, 5c, 6b, 7b, 8c, 9c, 10a
Similar or different?: 1d, 2s, 3d, 4d, 5d, 6s

Passage 9: *Auction sales*
Ideas: 1a, 2d, 3c, 4d, 5b, 6b, 7a, 8b, 9c, 10a
Vocabulary: 1d, 2a, 3a, 4b, 5c, 6a, 7b, 8a, 9b, 10b
Missing word summary: 1b, 2b, 3c, 4a, 5a, 6c, 7b

Passage 10: *The planemakers*
Ideas: 1c, 2a, 3b, 4d, 5b, 6d, 7d, 8a, 9c, 10c
Vocabulary: 1c, 2b, 3a, 4a, 5c, 6b, 7c, 8a, 9c, 10c
Similar or different?: 1s, 2s, 3d, 4s, 5s, 6d

Passage 11: *Dreams – what do they mean?*
Ideas: 1f, 2t, 3t, 4f, 5f, 6f, 7f, 8t, 9t, 10t
Vocabulary: 1b, 2a, 3a, 4c, 5b, 6b, 7c, 8a, 9c, 10a
Spot the topic: 1b, 2a, 3c, 4a, 5b, 6c

Passage 12: *To be or not to be a vegetarian*
Ideas: 1c, 2b, 3d, 4b, 5c, 6c, 7c, 8a, 9c, 10c
Vocabulary: 1b, 2d, 3a, 4c, 5a, 6c, 7b, 8c, 9b, 10c
Missing word summary: 1b, 2b, 3b, 4a, 5b, 6c, 7c, 8c

Passage 13: *Making leather*
Ideas: 1b, 2b, 3c, 4b, 5b, 6c, 7b, 8a, 9a, 10c
Vocabulary: 1d, 2d, 3a, 4a, 5c, 6a, 7a, 8c, 9c, 10a
Similar or different?: 1s, 2s, 3d, 4d, 5d, 6d

Passage 14: *Cats*
Ideas: 1d, 2b, 3a, 4b, 5c, 6a, 7a, 8c, 9b, 10b
Vocabulary: 1d, 2a, 3b, 4a, 5c, 6d, 7c, 8a, 9a, 10b
Spot the topic: 1b, 2c, 3a, 4c, 5a

Passage 15: *The history of chemistry*
Ideas: 1b, 2a, 3a, 4b, 5d, 6b, 7a, 8b, 9c, 10b
Vocabulary: 1a, 2b, 3c, 4a, 5d, 6b, 7b, 8d, 9a, 10c
Missing word summary: 1c, 2a, 3b, 4c, 5a, 6a, 7b, 8b

Passage 16: *Electric fish*
Ideas: 1t, 2f, 3t, 4t, 5f, 6f, 7t, 8f, 9t, 10f
Vocabulary: 1b, 2b, 3a, 4b, 5a, 6d, 7a, 8b, 9a, 10a
Similar or different?: 1d, 2d, 3s, 4d, 5d, 6s, 7s, 8s

Passage 17: *Dried food*
Ideas: 1c, 2b, 3d, 4b, 5b, 6b, 7b, 8a, 9b, 10a
Vocabulary: 1a, 2a, 3b, 4c, 5a, 6a, 7d, 8b, 9c, 10b
Spot the topic: 1c, 2a, 3b, 4c, 5a

Passage 18: *The United Nations*
Ideas: 1c, 2d, 3a, 4b, 5c, 6a, 7b, 8d, 9a, 10c
Vocabulary: 1a, 2a, 3b, 4d, 5c, 6a, 7a, 8b, 9d, 10a
Similar or different?: 1s, 2d, 3s, 4s, 5d

Passage 19: *Pottery*
Ideas: 1d, 2c, 3a, 4d, 5b, 6c, 7d, 8c, 9b, 10c
Vocabulary: 1c, 2a, 3b, 4c, 5b, 6b, 7a, 8b, 9c, 10b
Similar or different?: 1d, 2s, 3s, 4s, 5d, 6d

Passage 20: *Pasteurization*
Ideas: 1f, 2t, 3t, 4t, 5f, 6f, 7f, 8f, 9t, 10f
Vocabulary: 1c, 2c, 3b, 4b, 5b, 6b, 7a, 8a, 9a, 10a
Spot the topic: 1a, 2a, 3a, 4b, 5a

Passage 21: *Modern surgery*
Ideas: 1a, 2a, 3a, 4c, 5c, 6a, 7c, 8c, 9a, 10a
Vocabulary: 1a, 2c, 3c, 4a, 5b, 6b, 7a, 8b, 9c, 10c
Similar or different?: 1s, 2d, 3s, 4d, 5d

Passage 22: *Smoking and cancer*
Ideas: 1f, 2f, 3t, 4t, 5t, 6t, 7t, 8f, 9f, 10f
Vocabulary: 1a, 2c, 3c, 4a, 5c, 6a, 7a, 8b, 9a, 10b
Missing word summary: 1c, 2b, 3c, 4b, 5a, 6c, 7b, 8b

Passage 23: *Rabies*
Ideas: 1f, 2t, 3t, 4t, 5t, 6t, 7t, 8f, 9f, 10f
Vocabulary: 1b, 2a, 3a, 4c, 5b, 6a, 7a, 8c, 9a, 10c
Spot the topic: 1b, 2a, 3a, 4c, 5c

Passage 24: *Vitamins*
Ideas: 1c, 2c, 3a, 4c, 5a, 6a, 7b, 8d, 9b, 10a
Vocabulary: 1c, 2a, 3c, 4a, 5a, 6c, 7c, 8a, 9a, 10a
Similar or different?: 1s, 2s, 3s, 4d, 5d, 6s

Passage 25: *Bringing up children (1)*
Ideas: 1t, 2f, 3t, 4f, 5t, 6t, 7f, 8t, 9t, 10t
Vocabulary: 1a, 2c, 3b, 4c, 5c, 6a, 7a, 8b, 9a, 10a
Missing word summary: 1a, 2c, 3b, 4c, 5a, 6b, 7c, 8a

Passage 26: *Bringing up children (2)*
Ideas: 1b, 2a, 3a, 4c, 5d, 6d, 7c, 8b, 9a 10b
Vocabulary: 1d, 2a, 3b, 4a, 5c, 6b, 7c, 8a, 9b, 10a
Spot the topic: 1c, 2a, 3b, 4a

Passage 27: *Etiquette (Part 1)*
Ideas: 1f, 2t, 3f, 4f, 5f, 6f, 7t, 8t, 9f, 10t
Vocabulary: 1b, 2a, 3c, 4a, 5c, 6c, 7a, 8b, 9c, 10a
Similar or different?: 1s, 2d, 3s, 4d, 5s, 6d

Passage 28: *Etiquette (Part 2)*
Ideas: 1b, 2d, 3b, 4b, 5b, 6a, 7c, 8c, 9d, 10a
Vocabulary: 1c, 2a, 3a, 4c, 5b, 6a, 7c, 8a, 9b, 10d
Missing word summary: 1b, 2c, 3b, 4a, 5b, 6c, 7a, 8a

Passage 29: *Social classes (Part 1)*
Ideas: 1d, 2b, 3b, 4b, 5c, 6c, 7c, 8a, 9c, 10a
Vocabulary: 1b, 2c, 3a, 4c, 5c, 6d, 7a, 8d, 9a, 10c
Spot the topic: 1a, 2c, 3b, 4a, 5c

Passage 30: *Social classes (Part 2)*
Ideas: 1d, 2b, 3a, 4b, 5c, 6c, 7a, 8c, 9b, 10a
Vocabulary: 1d, 2b, 3a, 4d, 5a, 6c, 7b, 8c, 9c, 10d
Similar or different?: 1s, 2d, 3d, 4s, 5s, 6d, 7s